Letts **STUDY GUIDE**

AGE 11-14

KEY STAGE 3

TECHNOLOGY

Keith West and Paul Smith

- A clear introduction to the new National Curriculum

- Topic by topic coverage, with lots of diagrams and illustrations

- Activities and projects, designed to encourage active learning

- Frequent questions to test your knowledge

- Index and glossary of terms

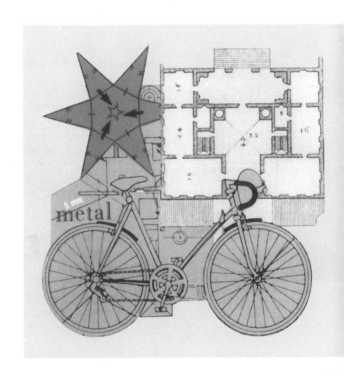

First published 1991
Reprinted 1991, 1992
Revised 1995

Letts Educational
Aldine House
Aldine Place
London W12 8AW
Tel: 0181-743 7514

Illustrations: Ian Foulis Associates, Kevin Jones, Michael Renouf, Tek-Art, Artistic License
© BPP (Letts Educational) Ltd 1995

British Library Cataloguing in Publication Data
A CIP record for this book is available from the British Library

ISBN 1 85758 349 3

Acknowledgements
The authors would like to thank the following people: Isabel Kirby, Pamela Lucas, Tony Pearson, Trevor Robinson, Arran Smith and Lee Trueman for allowing the use of their design work; Colin Austen, Jean Crossley and Mick Lynch for helpful comments and advice; Joyce Smith and Sandra Richardson for their excellent word processing; and finally their wives, Andrea and Linda, for their tolerance and support.

The authors and publishers are grateful to the following for permission to reproduce photographs and text extracts in this book:

p31 Ian Thraves; p39 The Daily Telegraph Picture Library; p72 Humber Bridge Board; pp75–6 microwave operating instructions reproduced by permission of Panasonic UK; p104 'West lets the sun shine in' by Michael Hulme, The Guardian, © The Guardian 1990; p108 Commotion Ltd; p140 (bottom) Popperfoto/Reuter; p153 DACS for permission to reproduce: Persistence of Memory by Salvador Dali © DEMART PRO ARTE B/V DACS 1991, Golconde by Rene Magritte © ADAGP, Paris and DACS, London 1991; p153 The Bridgeman Art Library; p168 photos by Steven Behr, © Stockfile; p173 text and photos reproduced by permission of the Humber Bridge Board.

Material from the National Curriculum is Crown copyright and is reproduced by permission of the Controller of HMSO.

Every effort has been made to trace copyright holders and to obtain their permission for the use of copyright material. The authors and publishers will gladly receive information enabling them to rectify any error or omission in subsequent editions.

Printed and bound in Great Britain by Livesey Ltd, Shrewsbury

Letts Educational is the trading name of BPP (Letts Educational) Ltd.

Contents

*I*ntroduction

S UCCESSFUL STUDYING AT KEY STAGE 3

During Key Stage 3 of the National Curriculum, you will have to study the following subjects:

English, mathematics, science, technology, a modern foreign language (usually French or German), geography and history. If you go to school in Wales, you will also be required to learn Welsh.

This stage of your education is very important because it lays the foundation which you will need to embark upon your GCSE courses. The National Curriculum requires you and all 11–14 year olds to follow the same programmes of study, which define the knowledge and skills you will need to learn and develop during your course.

At school, your teachers will be monitoring your progress. At the end of Key Stage 3, your performance will be assessed and you will be given a National Curriculum level. Most students should reach level 5 or level 6, some may reach levels 7 or 8, or perhaps even higher. In English, mathematics and science, you will have to take a National Test towards the end of your last year at Key Stage 3. The results of your tests, also marked in levels, will be set alongside your teachers' assessment of your work to give an overall picture of how you have done.

How this book will help you

This book is designed for you to use at home to support the work you are doing at school. Think of it as a companion or study guide to help you prepare for class work and homework. Inside the book, you will find the level descriptions which will be used to assess your performance. We have included them in the book so that, as you near the end of Key Stage 3, you will be able to check how well you are doing.

Reading the book, and doing the questions and activities will help you get to grips with the most important elements of the National Curriculum. Before you begin to read the book itself, take a few moments to read the introductory sections on 'Technology in the National Curriculum' and 'How to use this book'.

T ECHNOLOGY IN THE NATIONAL CURRICULUM

Your progress in technology is measured by your achievement in two different Attainment Targets (ATs).

AT1: Design
AT2: Making

You will also be expected to show some information technology capability.

You may wonder what you will be doing as you study for Key Stage 3 technology. Basically it is very simple. You will study existing technological things and identify problems and needs for which you can provide the solutions. You will be expected to gather information from a range of sources including talking and writing to other people. You are expected to recognize your own problems and opportunities and create your own solutions to them.

After you have identified an opportunity you must use your judgment to generate the best designed solution. You may need to make tests and conduct experiments and before making a finished product it may be necessary to make a working model. You will be expected to take into account such things as cost time, available skill and the number of items you intend to produce. You must be prepared to consider other ideas and accept that your first idea is not always the best one. When you make your designs you will need to plan the manufacture carefully. You may need to take advice from others. As you make your products you will use your knowledge of tools, equipment and materials and you will be expected to work safely.

Try to evaluate your work as you proceed, being careful to record your reasoning and decisions. Be careful to consider materials, equipment, manufacturing techniques and function. A good technologist is always looking for improvements. You will find ways to evaluate your work but it is important that you decide in advance precisely what you are attempting. You will then be able to judge your outcome by comparing it with what you had decided to set out to do.

You will be using information technology (IT) in almost every other subject that you study in school. In technology, however, you will explore the full range of uses of IT, including data bases, modelling and control technology. You will also have to consider the limitations of IT. The emphasis will always be on your using hardware and software to its fullest extent.

Don't be too worried though, if some of this is unfamiliar to you at the moment. The National Curriculum is designed to develop your understanding as you progress through the different levels in each Attainment Target. This book will help you to do well.

H OW TO USE THIS BOOK

Before proceeding further, carefully read the first three chapters of this book. They will give you invaluable help and will explain simply what otherwise might appear to you a complicated subject. Throughout these chapters, the *Now test yourself* questions will check your understanding. The answers are given at the end of each chapter. The *Young technologist at work* exercises will pose more practical problems for consideration.

In Chapter 4 you will be given a series of assignments to do. Half of these have possible answers provided, whereas the others just have clues to help you. In general, it is best to remember that there is no, one, completely 'correct' answer to most technological problems. Most solutions will have merit but some will be better than others!

There are also five longer assignments to work through. These are different from the shorter assignments in two important ways. Firstly, they are not focused on just one Attainment Target (AT). Instead they are wide-ranging and require all the AT skills. Secondly, they are not intended to represent only one particular level of study and learning. You can give as little or as much depth as you wish. These longer assignments will help you best if you tackle them towards the end of the Key Stage.

This book is, in effect, a 'course companion'. It should complement the schoolwork you do. It will give you confidence in dealing with various technology problems. You will become familiar with the design process and be capable of making things that work! Furthermore, by practising these skills you will foster your own design creativity.

CHAPTER 1

Designing

I NTRODUCTION

There are a variety of ways of tackling design activities. Engineers, furniture makers, chefs, artists and playwrights all engage in the design process but each approaches it in a different way.

 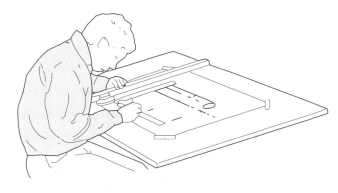

You can consider all these different approaches as points along a line (a continuum). At one end you can put the expressive/creative aspects of design (artists and playwrights). At the other you can put the engineers who are mainly concerned with function and need.

Artists _____ Engineers

To try to describe the thought processes and activities of artists is very difficult. It seems that their ideas for work (their inspiration) arise from a reaction between the subject, handling the materials and the emotions and feelings of the creator. The engineer, on the other hand, works in a more straightforward way. This is because there are definite problems or needs that have to be resolved.

The young technologist at work

Consider this list of 'designers':

Fashion designer	Hairstylist	Electrical engineer
Chef	Public transport organizer	Poet
Jewellery maker	Furniture maker	Advertising agent

On the scale below, write in the appropriate space where you think each one falls on the design continuum. To help you, three of the 'designers' have been added to the scale already.

Artists		Hairstylist			Fashion designer			Furniture maker		Engineers

---

The purpose of this exercise is to help you understand that different aspects of design demand different approaches. It is important to adopt the approach most suitable for a particular situation.

The problem-solving approach

You can consider the extremes of the design continuum in terms of what the designers do.

During your early years at school you may remember that quite a lot of time was given to the expressive and creative aspects of design – creative writing, painting and claywork, for example. It is less likely that you spent much time on problem-solving activities. The next section explains in some detail the problem-solving approach to design.

If this approach is broken down you will be able to see a sequence of logical activities which can lead to successful conclusions. Experience in this step-by-step approach is essential if you are to develop 'design capability'. After some time you will find yourself thinking along these lines automatically, indeed you may find yourself thinking about two stages simultaneously.

Sometimes it is possible to think of solutions instantly but you have to guard against this. First ideas are very rarely the best. In any event, having an idea is not designing. It only becomes design when the idea is developed, refined, modified, tested and assessed.

The stages of the design process

The design process can be broken down into several stages:

1. The problem or need.

2. The design brief.

3. Thinking.

4. Researching.

5. Developing ideas (imaging).

6. Planning.

7. Making.

8. Testing.

9. Judging.

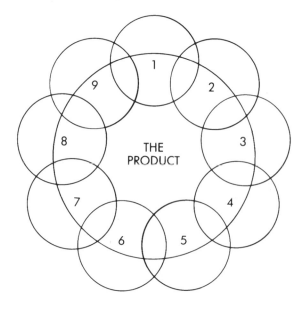

Each stage is not independent of the others as each is linked to the one before and after it. All stages contribute to the final product and it is likely that if you were to remove one of the stages the process would be incomplete.

Attainment Targets (AT)

The Attainment Targets in technology are:

AT 1 Designing

AT 2 Making

D ESIGNING SKILLS

The problem or need

This is where you start. It is important to be able to see clearly the need for design activities. For example, not being able to find a particular musical track in a collection of recorded cassettes indicates a need for some kind of filing system.

Similarly, a handicapped person moving into a new home may have difficulty using electrical appliances if all the wall sockets are mounted close to the floor.

Design brief

The design brief is a way of expressing the problem in a clear and concise way. The person who supplies the brief should give as much information as possible, particularly on limiting factors such as cost and available time.

It is important that you write the brief for yourself. It's rather like asking questions and then having to give an appropriate answer. Writing briefs will help you to clarify in your own mind the nature of the problem. Briefs must give all the available information in the form of points to be considered.

Generating a design

This is about 'thinking', 'researching', 'imaging' (picturing) and selecting solutions to problems. Starting with the design brief, you should form a list of the points to be considered. These can be in any order but thinking them out with the aid of an 'ARME' may help. This is described below.

Thinking

Aims: What is the precise function or functions of the object?

Resources: How much time is there?
What materials are available?
What equipment is available?
What skills are required?

Methods: Where can information be found?
How can the object be made?
Will its looks be acceptable?
Can it be made to work?

Evaluation: Does it fit the user's needs?
Will the object perform its function well?
What will be the effects of its use?
Who would be able to assess its success?

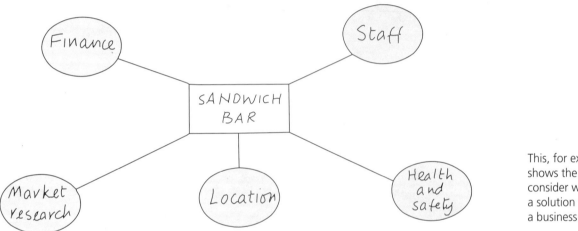

This, for example, shows the points to consider when seeking a solution to organizing a business

As you answer the above questions you are sure to find that others present themselves. Sometimes you will find that you cannot fully answer a question. When that is the case you will need to obtain more information or seek the help of others.

Researching

The vital question then is where to get the necessary help from. You will need to identify appropriate sources of information that will help.

There are many sources which you could turn to but the ones you choose will depend on the precise information you need. The following list comments briefly on the main sources of information:

Textbooks

These are a valuable source of reference. They will give you relevant examples of how other people have found solutions to problems. They are also a very useful source of technical information.

Teachers

They have a lot of practical experience in solving problems and they are aware of the difficulties under which you will be working. They will be able to give you practical and realistic advice. A modern method of helping students is the 'nudge and wink' approach where the teacher prompts and guides the students into a worthwhile course of action without actually telling them what to do. Don't expect your teacher to do the work and make your decisions for you!

Experts

Apart from your teachers, there are other people with expertise in the design field. For example, it might be possible to talk to people working in the research department of a local firm. There might also be local crafts people who could be of help. Potters, furniture makers and textile workers are some of the obvious ones but there are many others. Regional Arts Councils keep up-to-date records of all practising crafts people.

Libraries

A useful place for research is a library because it will contain a wide range of sources of information. Most public libraries have a reference section where specialist magazines, as well as books, are available. Examples of those currently available are:

Arts Review
Ceramic Review (pottery)
Computer Weekly
Design
Essentials (general textiles)
Model Engineers' Workshop
Modelling International
PC User
The Woodworker

You will also find that the library staff will be very helpful in giving you information about the availability and location of the sources, providing you explain precisely what it is you need to know.

Museums

In design, it is often a good idea to start with an existing, or earlier, solution to a problem. A museum may have exhibits which might give you new ideas, and the variety of materials used could enable you to look at things in a new way. There are also specialist collections of items which show the development of design over time. For example, a display could show the development of tools from primitive tools made from animal bones to heavy cast iron tools right through to modern light plastic ones. Similarly, there might be a display on how the impressionist painters produced their works of art.

Information centres

As well as libraries and museums, which provide general information over a wide range of topics, there are also specialist organizations which can be very helpful.

These include:

Citizens Advice Bureaux
Tourist Information Offices
Health Centres
The Consumers' Association
The Design Centre

Using the sources

When using any of the above you should make notes of the information collected. This is particularly important as later you may need to refer back to the information either to clarify or to add to your original research. You should try to consult more than one source even if the first one seems to give you what you want because it is rare to get all you want from the first source. Some sources, of course, may not be able to help at all but they could point you in the right direction by instructing you where you could acquire information.

When undertaking research estimate approximately how long it will take you to do the necessary reading and so on. Then double your time allocation, as you will usually spend twice as long as you had originally expected.

Try to be very strict with yourself and make sure you do not get distracted as you may find that, once you get started with your researching, you will be tempted to wander off into areas and things that you do not know about and which look or sound interesting, but which are not that relevant to your task. So you need to keep asking yourself, 'Is this relevant?'

NOTES FOR MY TECHNOLOGY PROJECT
From: The Ways of the World,
I. Jivd, Box Press, 1994

Every year, the average family of four will throw away the equivalent of six trees, fifty kilograms of metal and forty kilograms of plastics

Imaging

With all the relevant information gathered together you can now start to develop your own ideas or solutions. It is very rare these days for people to have completely new ideas. More often they are developments of existing ideas. This is perfectly acceptable as long as you have developed a new interpretation of an idea and not simply copied an existing solution.

Designs are usually worked out on paper by using drawings, notes, flow charts, story-boards, diagrams, and so on. IT IS ESSENTIAL TO RECORD ALL IDEAS AND DEVELOPMENTS. This is because this helps you to work out your ideas and to share and discuss your ideas with other people. Another reason is that it provides evidence of your thought processes. These thought processes are probably more important than the final product and for this reason there is a special section on design sheets starting on page 14.

Recording an idea: the use of story-boards for the advertising of a new product – 'Fresho-mint toothpaste'

Finally, it should be emphasized that this part of the process is probably the most important of them all. Time spent on refining ideas and production methods will pay off in the end. It is certainly much easier and cheaper to correct mistakes on paper rather than in the specified material. Once the design has been finalized it is worth making a last check by comparing your idea with the original design brief.

Evaluating

Testing

Trying out your solution to a problem is an important part of the design process. You should make checks during the production process before the final product is created but you must also test the completed solution more thoroughly at the end. Often the results of your testing can cause you to modify your design.

Judging

This is the final stage of any design process. It can be disappointing if you find that the finished product is not as satisfactory as you had hoped but if this is the case the experience can still be very useful by asking the question 'Why?'. Your answers will help you in future projects. It is always a good idea to involve other people at this stage to see if they agree with your solutions or findings. There may be a need for further modifications. Your product must be compared with the original design need or brief to see if it does exactly what is expected. Ask yourself the question 'How could it be more successful?'.

Don't forget to record your findings and answers to questions. You may realize that you have made mistakes either in design or in the use of your time. Recording these facts will help you avoid making the same mistakes again.

THE PURPOSE OF DESIGN SHEETS

Why bother with a design sheet? You might already know what you want to make and have a note of the sizes. Why not just go ahead and make it?

There are several reasons why you need to modify your ideas throughout a design sheet. Design sheets can serve different functions. It is important for you to understand what they are. This will help you to make the best use of your design sheets.

First ideas

The first and most important function of a design sheet is for you to communicate the visual information to yourself. This helps you picture your design in your mind's eye. The first design is most important. It might not be your best idea but it will contain the seed of your thinking that will lead to more successful ideas. At this stage you should concern yourself only with communicating information to yourself. It is important that you are able to understand your own drawings but you should not worry too much about the standard of presentation. You may be the only person who sees these first designs so the main thing is to get down as much information as you can.

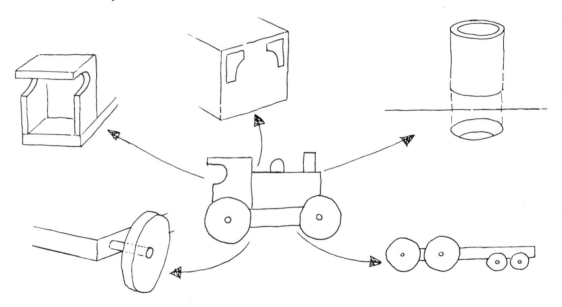

Asking questions

Once you have given yourself the chance to visualize your ideas it is time to think about the second function of a design sheet. You should now ask yourself many questions. These questions will be grouped into two types:

1. Specific questions relating to the brief.
2. General questions.

The specific questions arise from the design specifications and will be different for each problem. These specific questions would in turn give rise to general questions such as:

Would it be better if it was:

taller?	thicker?
thinner?	smaller?
darker?	stronger?
more stable?	more colourful or had different colours?

These questions surround the second stage or function of design sheets. When you draw your ideas you provide the opportunity to refine them. Your first idea is very rarely your best. It has to be refined until you are sure that it is not possible to improve upon it any further. When this stage is reached you can, if necessary, go on to consider the third and final reason for producing design sheets.

Communication and presentation

Another function of your design sheets is to communicate information to other people. In the early stages your drawings do not need to be very clear and you can use your own imagination in order to visualize the details which are lacking on them. This is possible because **you** know what you want your design to look like. When you communicate visual information to other people you must be much more careful. Not only do you have to give as much information as possible but you also have to 'sell' your idea to them. This means you have to present your idea in as precise and pleasant a way as possible.

As a member of the public it is these final design sheets you most often see. It is these sheets that designers use to show off both their design and presentation skills. The design world is highly competitive. This makes the standard of design and design sheets very high. However, it is always worthwhile remembering that some of the most successful designs started life very humbly indeed, being first drawn on the back of a cigarette packet, or in one very famous case, on the side of a garage wall!

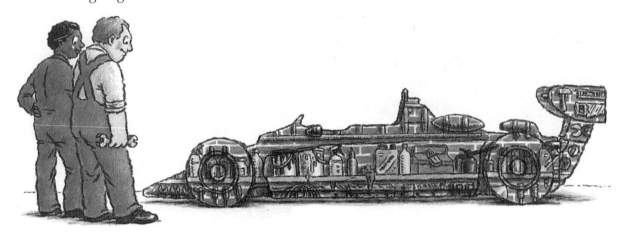

So, design sheets serve three very useful important functions. These are:

❶ To help you imagine your design.
❷ To help you refine your diagram.
❸ To communicate this information to other people.

❶ and ❷ are particularly important and should receive your full attention. ❸ is also important but it is very tempting to spend lots of time producing 'slick' or pretty design sheets which have ideas that are not so good or well thought out. In reality the three functions are not viewed separately. Your drawings will therefore serve all of them at the same time but to different extents.

E LEMENTS OF DESIGN – A VISUAL LANGUAGE

As you have read earlier, there are several approaches to design. If, for example, you were designing a shopping bag for a blind person you would need to develop a problem-solving approach. If, on the other hand, you wanted to paint a picture or write a poem about travelling in a time machine then it could not really be said that you were solving a problem. Instead it would be much better to describe your activity and approach as a kind of reaction between you, your feelings, your ideas, and the materials with which you are working. Overall, whatever kind of design activity you engage in it will probably be a combination of these different ways of thinking.

One thing is for certain: most design activities require you to deal with the visual elements that make up what can be called a visual 'language'. This language uses images to convey information rather than written or spoken statements. When you talk and write to people you use letters, words and sentences. In your visual language you use:

❶ Line.
❷ Shape and form.
❸ Texture.
❹ Composition.
❺ Colour.

The best way to understand these different elements is to look at the illustrations on the next few pages. It should then become clear that each of the illustrations has a definite 'quality' about it. These qualities are to do with line, shape and form, texture and colour. They can be seen in single qualities or in combination with one another. Their use will affect **contrast** and **harmony, composition** and **mood.**

Line

Lines can be used to create drawings. They do this by describing shapes and giving things a sense of direction. There are many types of line, each having a different quality. Lines can be sharp and precise or soft and gentle. They can be faint or dark, thick or thin.

Lots of thick black lines

Soft lines in the foreground

Shape and form

These are two other elements of this visual language. Shapes are two-dimensional, they exist on the surface of things. Squares and circles are geometric shapes. When they are given a third dimension, that is depth, then squares become cubes and circles become spheres. So now shapes become forms. Shapes and forms can be considered in lots of different ways. One convenient way of thinking about them is under the headings of:

(a) Regular shapes and forms
(b) Irregular shapes and forms

Lines and shapes

Shapes and forms

(a) *Regular shapes and forms*

These are predictable and include geometric shapes and shapes that are symmetrical (see glossary on page 175). Regular shapes occur in both nature and the made world. They are probably more common in the made world. People who live in the western part of the world favour regular shapes which form predictable patterns. In cultures from other parts of the world, such as the Far East, people prefer irregularity and asymmetrical patterns.

Regular

(b) *Irregular shapes and forms*

These are different from those described above because they do not have lines of symmetry. In this respect they are said to be asymmetrical. Irregular shapes are much more common in nature than in the made world and are usually more interesting to look at.

Irregular

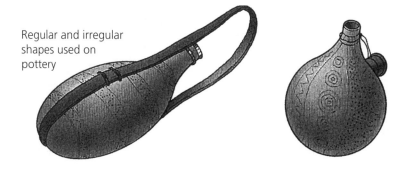

Regular and irregular shapes used on pottery

When dealing with the subject of different shapes there is an important question to ask. This is whether or not the shapes relate to one another in terms of the features they have in common. Shapes which do have things in common can be said to be of the same family. This means they will probably look 'right' in combination with one another.

Combining shapes from different visual families on the other hand would be like putting cats and dogs together and expecting them to get on well. Consider this illustration and see how the unrelated shapes create visual problems:

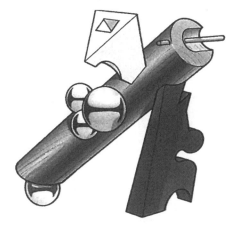

Another way you can consider shape and form is as positives and negatives. Positive shapes and forms are those that can be described as being solid whereas the shapes seen as 'gaps' in between a group of objects can be described as being negative.

This photograph shows a collection of both positive and negative shapes. See how sometimes the negative shapes look the more interesting.

The young technologist at work

Take a group of objects and consider the shapes that exist between them.
Are they positive or negative?

Texture

Texture can be real and apparent. It is to do with surface pattern and the way a surface feels. All objects have texture. It can be very smooth like glass or silk or it can be very rough like jagged rock or the bark of some trees.

Erosion and the build up of sea creatures created this texture

Textures become part of an object as the object is created. This is true of both made and natural objects. The making process produces the texture.

Natural textures found on the sea shore

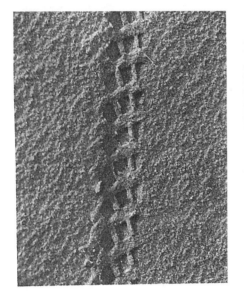

Man made textures found on the sea shore

Let's consider building bricks. Originally, when bricks were made by hand, they were slightly uneven and rough. Then, as the making technology improved, it became possible to make each brick exactly the same size and perfectly smooth. Now the technology, which is even more advanced, is used to make the bricks uneven and slightly rough again. This is because it is now appreciated that slight variations in size and texture help to make objects more interesting.

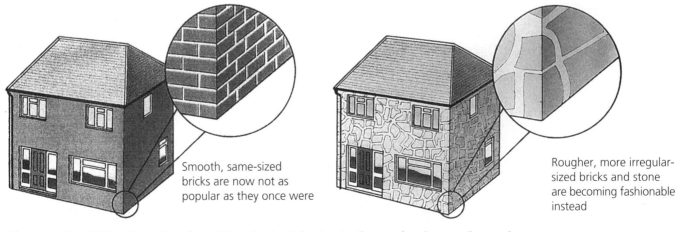

Smooth, same-sized bricks are now not as popular as they once were

Rougher, more irregular-sized bricks and stone are becoming fashionable instead

Texture should be thought of as either incised (cut into the surface) or embossed (built up onto the surface). When used in combination with one another they provide three layers on which to work.

Texture is, however, not only what you can feel, it is also what you see. This is because of the reflections and shadows created in the surface. Differences in colour can exaggerate surface texture. Printed surfaces can also create texture. Potato and lino printing are two techniques which can create surface pattern and texture.

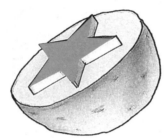 

In design, contrast is one of the most useful elements of the visual language. This is because contrast can be used to draw the viewer's attention. It also affects the way things are seen. If, for example, you like to wear and be seen in grey, strangely enough you wouldn't wear everything in a particular outfit in grey! Instead you would wear one of the items in a different colour. This has the effect of contrasting the colours and draws attention to both – one being the grey!

Another example of the successful use of contrast is in pottery. If you had developed a very effective texture and were going to decorate a pot with it a successful approach would be to apply the texture next to a very smooth area. This again would contrast the texture and in so doing draw attention to it. This would be far more effective than covering the whole pot with the same texture.

Composition

Composition is the way that everything you have just been reading about is combined into pictures and designs so that they complement each other and the overall product looks good. It is a complicated aspect to consider because it deals with all the elements that make up visual language and the ways they react with one another. Like design, good composition arises from much trial and experimentation. On many occasions you will make successful decisions about composition and layout without knowing why. But if you feel that it looks right, it probably is!

Look at the photograph of the cyclist. See how line, shape and form, texture and composition combine to give the photo impact.

On the next page are two exercises in photographic composition. This kind of artwork was developed by the artist David Hockney who called the technique 'joiners'. Instead of taking one big photograph of a scene or event the idea is to take lots of little ones and then join them together. By doing this you have the opportunity of creating a composition which combines time with all the other elements of visual language.

If you look carefully at the composition of the hot air balloon example you can see that the photographs show different stages of the balloon's flight. The second illustration is of an old school entrance which has been photographed from several different angles. This produces a view of the building which it is impossible to find in 'real life'. The fact that several images appear more than once is deliberate.

Both pictures contain all the elements of the visual language that you have been reading about. Look carefully at both of the compositions and see if you can work out how and in what way each of the elements has been used.

Now test yourself

PHOTO-JOINERS

The balloon

1   Although these photographs were taken at different times during the preparation and flight of this balloon you should be able to see something that links them together. What is it?

2 and 3   Look at the picture as a whole and see if you can identify two shapes that re-occur constantly. One is in the top half of the picture. You should be able to 'spot' a second shape that re-occurs in the machinery.

4   Consider what colours would be suitable for the balloon and with the aid of the colour wheel (see page 27) decide on what coloured card the composition should be mounted.

The school building

1   Look at this composition and see if you can understand what it is that creates the feeling of depth or distance in the picture.

2 and 3   You should also be able to say what parts of the picture were of particular interest to the artist and how your attention is drawn to them.

4   Consider line, pattern, texture and shape then arrange them in the order of importance in this picture.

Answers are given on page 41

Apart from having favourite colours people also have opinions about what colours should appear together. Sometimes they are heard to say that they dislike a colour or that one particular colour is 'awful'. In fact there are no bad or awful colours. What people mean is that they dislike certain combinations of colours. Up to only a few years ago people in the western part of the world tended to wear very dull clothes and were careful to avoid bright colours. However, more recently there has been an explosion of colour. Now garments are created using a wide variety of different hues and shades. This shows that what is 'right' and 'wrong' in terms of colours is really up to individual taste and so you should wear the colours that you like best or which suit a particular occasion.

So, as you can see, all this suggests that colour is a very important part of design.

The spectrum – colours of light and colours of pigment

We see colours because light falls on things. When light passes through things such as rain it can be split up into its basic component colours. The result of this is called a rainbow. The splitting up of the white sunlight into an arrangement of different colours gives us the SPECTRUM. An easy way to remember the colours of the spectrum and the order in which they appear is by the following:

Richard	Red
Of	Orange
York	Yellow
Gave	Green
Battle	Blue
In	Indigo
Vain	Violet

Red, blue and green are called the primary colours. The other colours of the spectrum are created by mixing primary colours together. Colours created by mixing two primaries together are called secondary colours.

It is important that you know and understand the difference between colours of light and colours of pigment. Until recently artists and designers did not often work in colours of light. However, because of film, television and computer graphics, colours of light are now used quite a lot.

More often than using colours of light artists and designers use paint dyes, inks and stains. These are called colours of pigment (pigments are natural or synthetic coloured substances). In dealing with colours of pigment it is important to remember that the primary colours are red and blue (just as with light) but that the third primary colour is yellow. In both light and pigment when two primary colours are mixed together a secondary colour is created, and when a primary and a secondary colour are mixed a third group is created. This group is called tertiary colours.

The young technologist at work

THE COLOUR WHEEL

A lot of useful knowledge can be gained from looking at and making up the colour wheel shown below. When you choose to use colour in your design using the colour wheel will help you to decide which combinations of colours are the best to use.

Making the wheel

Trace the first drawing below onto a piece of card and cut it out. Then cut out the unshaded areas: Trace the colour wheel below and colour in the segments as indicated. Colour each segment so that the inner section is dark, the middle section is medium, and the outer section is light. Taking the disc, position it over the colour wheel so that a colour appears in the Key Colour hole. The wheel is now ready for use!

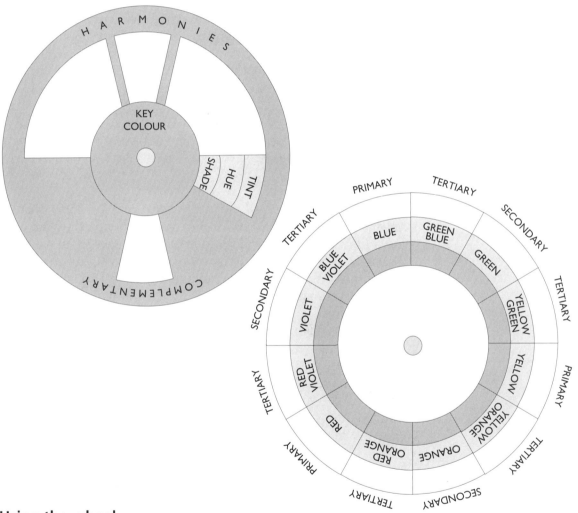

Using the wheel

Choose your key colour and move the disc until this colour appears in the Key Colour window. The colours that appear in the windows on either side of it are the harmonizing colours: the colours that work best with the key colour and with each other.

If you want to find the colour that contrasts with your key colour the greatest contrast is with the colour that appears in the window opposite the Key Colour window. These colours are called complementary colours.

Not all colours are included on the wheel but you will find that using the wheel will help you a lot.

Use of colour on design sheets

Now you have learnt a little about the theory of colour you should also try to learn a little about the practical aspects of using colour to improve the appearance and function of your drawings.

First of all consider the means by which you can apply colour. You can see from the list below that there are many ways in which you can produce coloured illustrations. These include:

- Drawing pencils.
- Pencil crayons.
- Wax crayons.
- Pastels.
- Coloured chalks and charcoal.
- Felt-tipped markers.
- Fibre-tipped markers.
- Inks.
- Paints.

An important thing to understand is that each of the above media (the materials in or with which you are working) has its own strengths and weaknesses. Some of the listed materials, for example, are very good for producing coloured lines but not very good for producing flat, even colour. On the other hand, some of the above media can cover big areas quickly but might be messy and difficult to control for fine, accurate lines.

If you have some of these materials you could try them out to see which you prefer. When you look at the examples of design sheets you will see how some of the materials have been used.

Drawing pencils and pencil and wax crayons are linear tools (that means they are good for producing lines) although they can be used to create areas of solid colour. One very successful way of using them is to apply light layers of different colours on top of each other. Another way when filling in areas with colour is to change frequently to a different shade or colour. Colours can appear to mix together this way. Don't try to rub or smudge the shading, it will only lose its 'freshness' and appear dirty. If you are working only with drawing pencils try to make sure you use a wide variety of strengths of shading, for example, from the very lightest shade of grey right down to the very darkest. Don't forget that the lightest shade you use is the paper itself! On heavily shaded areas a rubber or eraser can be used to rub out and so 'draw' white lines.

Pastels and chalks are interesting materials to work with. You need quite a rough paper to work them successfully. Smooth white paper is not really suitable but sugar papers can be used. You can achieve very smooth changes in colour with these materials but you must work from the top to the bottom of the picture and keep a piece of scrap paper between your hand and the drawing. Fill the biggest areas first leaving the smallest detail until last. When the colouring is complete you need to fix the work so that it does not smudge. Fixative does this best and can be bought from crafts shops but hairspray can be used as well. Remember to buy sprays which come in environment-friendly cans!

Felt-tipped and fibre-tipped markers have become very popular over recent years. Unless you have some very broad tipped markers these are also linear tools. Felt-tip drawings can look best when they appear to have been produced quite quickly. These pens are easy and clean to use although they can fade very quickly if exposed to direct sunlight. Letraset is one of the better quality brands which offer a very large range of shades. These can also be used with an air brush adaptor.

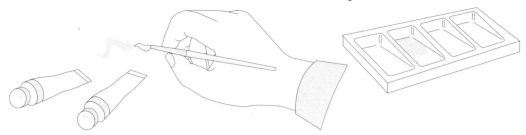

Coloured drawing inks are quite inexpensive and are interesting to use, especially with a 'dip pen'. Used in this way you can achieve a variety of good lines. You can also use drawing inks to cover large areas. This can be done with a soft brush and pure ink. Alternatively the ink can be diluted with water to make a wash. This will give a lighter tint of the same colour. Combinations of ink washes and fine pen drawings can be very effective. You may also be fortunate enough to use modern drawing pens such as 'Rapidographs'.

The disadvantage of inks is that they can be messy. Keep a scrap piece of paper handy and make sure you hold the bottle of ink with your spare hand. Unless the paper is soaked and stretched as you would do for water colour painting, ink washes will cause the paper to crinkle and crease.

Most people enjoy painting pictures but using *paints* on design sheets requires some skill and patience. Paints should be used with the minimum of water. Rest your hand on the working surface with your fingers close to the bristles. Always pull the brush along – never push it. Poster paints are the best for design. Again always work from the biggest areas first, leaving the detail until last.

Developing style and skill

You will already have a style to your drawing just as you have a style to your handwriting. The more drawing you do the more this style will develop.

It is common for students in their early teens to think they cannot draw. But there is a simple solution to this and this is to practise drawing continually. However, this drawing must be from objects that are 'real' and in front of you. Copying things from books is much less use.

There are a few tips that you can learn and a few tricks that you can use but the secret of drawing is learning to observe carefully. This is what is meant by the phrase 'a trained eye'!

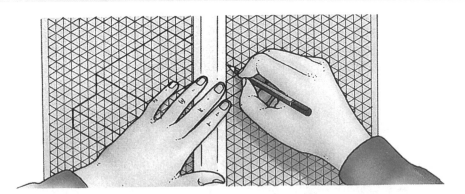

Isometric paper can be used to learn a little about three-dimensional drawings and how you should construct your drawings from centre lines and imaginary boxes. After a little practice using this kind of paper some of the basic rules that govern drawing in three dimensions will become clear. The rules for drawing in three dimensions (called 'perspective') are:

1. Vertical lines stay vertical.
2. Only lines that appear at the front of the picture and go away from you slope.
3. Lines that start above your eye level appear to slope downwards towards a vanishing point which is on the horizon.
4. Lines that start below your eye level (that means somewhere between your eyes and the ground) slope upwards towards the vanishing point.
5. The further these lines start from your eye level the more they slope.

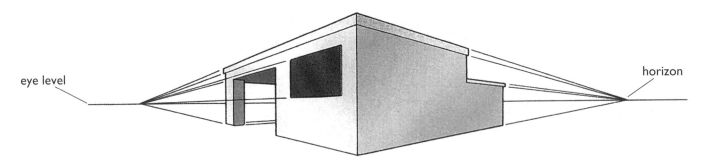

eye level   horizon

When constructing a drawing with lines do not make them too thick or heavy. If the drawing is then to be coloured or shaded the lines can (and should) be hidden in that they should disappear into the shading. So, when the drawing is complete, it should not be possible to distinguish the construction lines from the shading.

When you first learn to draw, three strengths of shading are all that you need: light, medium and dark. That is one for each side of the object you are drawing. Make sure the strongest contrasts and darker shading are used for the part of the object that is nearest to you. Shades which are most like each other should be used for the parts of the object that are furthest away from you.

Tip When shading keep all the lines going in the same direction.

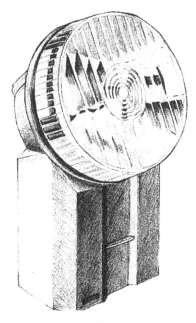

L EARNING FROM OTHER STUDENTS

Over the next few pages you will see a number of student projects illustrated.
These will help you to understand a little about the different approaches to design.

Building bridges

The use of models and prototypes

Building models is a good way of testing out your designs. Here Arran has
developed a design for a bridge building project. Having refined his ideas the student
then made the model very carefully. The testing involved recording the amount the
bridge moved when under stress. When loaded with 25 kg it moved 2 mm.

Working drawings

Illustrated with the bridge are the original design sheets. These are the 'first ideas'
sheets. Once an idea has been visualized it is necessary to plan with greater detail
and accuracy. Again this should be done using drawings. In the case of the bridge
these drawings were not merely pictorial, but were rough **orthographic projections.**

This method of drawing objects may seem complicated at first but it is very useful
because it provides other people with all the information in order for them to make
the object.

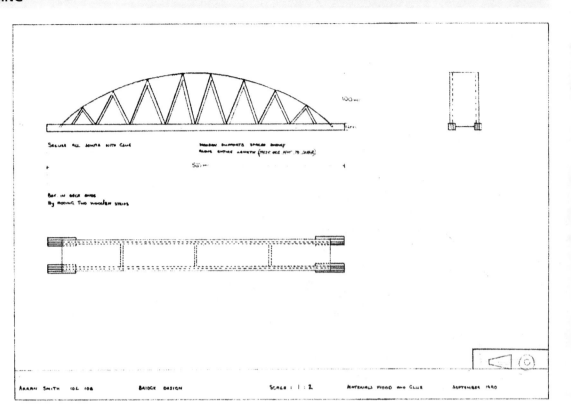

An orthographic drawing usually shows an object from three views. These are:
– a side elevation (a view of the object from the side)
– an end elevation (everything that can be seen of the object from one end)
– a plan view (a view of the object from above)

When you first start to produce these kinds of drawings you will find it helpful to produce them on graph paper. The correct way to do this is:

❶ Decide on the scale of your drawing so that it will fit on the paper.
❷ Draw a base line across the paper. The side and end elevations will stand on this.
❸ Draw two vertical lines. The distance apart will be the length of the object. These are the edges of the object as seen in the side and plan views.
❹ Draw a horizontal line above the base line. The distance apart should be equal to the height of the object.
❺ Draw a diagonal line through the corners of the graph squares (this will be at 45%). The line must be to the right of the lines drawn at stage 3.
❻ Draw two vertical lines to the right of the side elevation and long enough to meet the diagonal line in stage 5. The distance apart of these two lines will be the width of the object.
❼ Draw horizontal lines to meet the vertical lines at the point they touch the diagonal line.

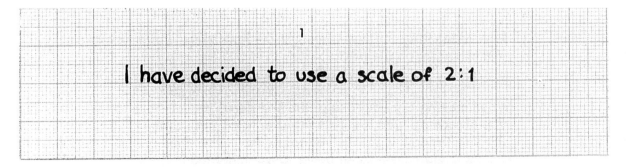

I have decided to use a scale of 2:1

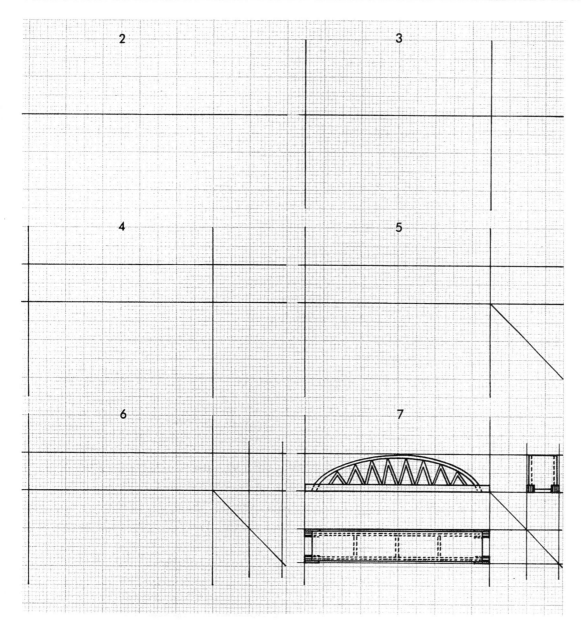

You have now completed the basic outline shape of your object.

Now look at the orthographic projection of the bridge on page 32 and see if you can 'read' the drawing. If the drawing has been produced properly it should be possible to gather enough information in order for the object to be made.

Model making

Before a model is made it has to be decided what it is to represent. Two types of model are:

1. Working models (these demonstrate how things work) like the steering mechanism on the tractor.
2. Static or visual models (these show how things will appear).

When making a model one of the first decisions you have to take concerns the type of material you are going to use. In the case of the bridge wood was used because strength was very important. However, if the model was just for looking at then it might have been better to use other materials such as card and plastic. This is because these materials are easier to work with than wood. Thin plastic can sometimes be cut with a craft knife or a pair of scissors.

A good place to enquire about model-making materials and techniques is your local model shop. Unlike big stores or supermarkets these model shops are usually staffed by enthusiasts who can give you a lot of help. Modelling exhibitions and clubs are also good places to see other people's work and to learn about techniques.

Apart from skills in building, modelling demands an inventive mind. This is because of the many discarded objects and materials that can be used to good effect. Some examples of this kind of thinking are:

– using natural sponge to imitate trees and shrubs (e.g. on model railways)
– using rice, pipe cleaners and fruit gums to imitate precious jewellery

An educational game

In this project Pam was asked to invent and produce a low-cost educational game that children would be actively involved with.

Out of this need Pam developed the idea of 'Dr Blake's Wildlife Activity Set'. You can see from the selection of design sheets and the products themselves that Pam has spent a great deal of time researching and making this project.

One of Pam's clever ideas was to create a character called Dr Blake who could act as a friend to the children using the game. Notice how he appears on the cards and that certain records have his seal of approval.

On the design sheets notice how Pam has used the same materials and techniques to illustrate her thought processes. However, when it comes to the actual product you can see that lots of different drawing and painting techniques have been used. This is a good way of creating interest through variety.

Another impressive aspect of this project is Pam's attention to detail. This includes the list of contents on the back of the box, the wire, wooden ring and detailed instructions for the mobile. All this, coupled with the zebra striped pencil, has helped to create a very well thought out and carefully made project.

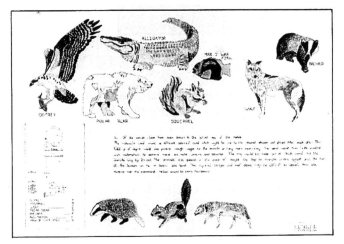
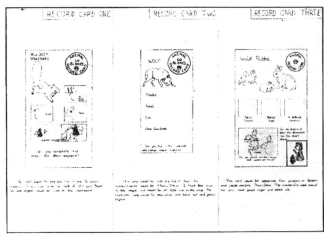

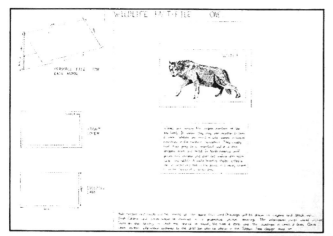

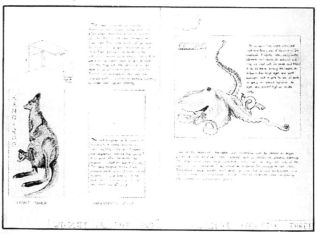

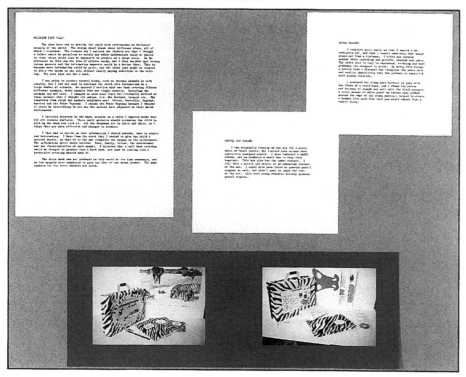

Lotus errant

It can be seen from the illustrations that the student, Lee, is interested in transport design. This is Lee's A Level examination project. As you study the design sheets see that Lee has worked in the same way as outlined earlier in this book.

Lee began this project by considering his examination needs to research a design project. This gave him the idea of designing a new type of vehicle for a sports car manufacturer. As a result of this investigation Lee decided to design an 'off road' vehicle for Lotus who normally only make sports cars.

Sheets 1, 2 and 3 show how Lee first looked in detail at the cars Lotus have made up to the present. This gave Lee a good feeling for the style of Lotus cars.

Sheets 4 and 5 contain the detailed specification that Lee considered. Sheet 5 is called an 'influences' sheet. The idea of this was to gather together pictures of items which Lee liked and would therefore influence his ideas.

Sheet 6 is very important because it shows Lee's first ideas. These appear in the bottom half of the sheet. Look particularly in the right hand corner, here you will see his first idea of the Lotus Errant.

From these first ideas came the final design which can be seen as presentation drawings on sheets 7 and 8. You can see that a great deal of care has been taken in the production of these drawings. Images of the car are seen from lots of interesting angles.

Sheets 9 and 10 deal with the inside of the vehicle and show that Lee has thought about lots of the detail such as the shape of the seats, the position of the seat belts as well as the style of the instruments and controls.

In order to produce drawings of this quality Lee had to develop a number of special drawing techniques. These techniques will give Lee a good start to his studies for a degree in transport design.

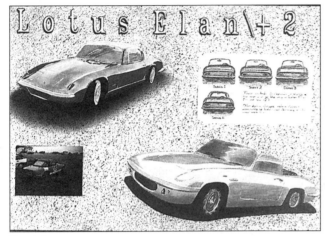

Sheet 1

Sheet 2

Sheet 3

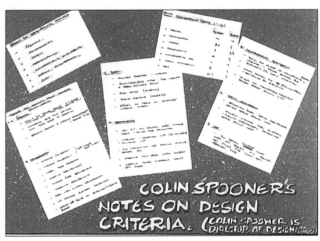

Sheet 4

Sheet 5

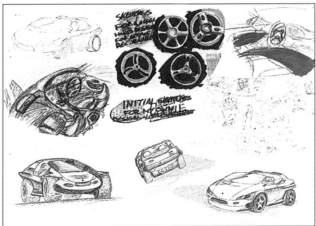

Sheet 6

Sheet 7

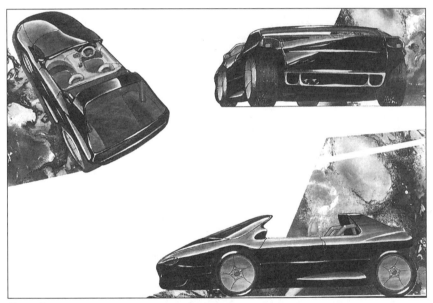

Sheet 8

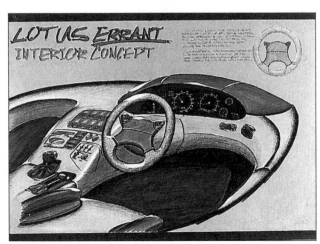

Sheet 9

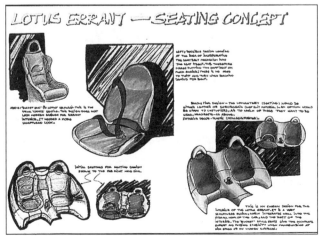

Sheet 10

L EARNING FROM THE EXPERTS

LEONARDO DA VINCI

Of all the famous designers there has been one person who stands out as a genius in many areas of design. This person is Leonardo da Vinci. He stands above all others because he brought together all kinds of knowledge in his work. His approach speaks to us over the centuries and is still relevant today.

Leonardo lived from 1452 to 1519, working mainly in Italy. He developed great skill and became famous as an artist and a scientist as well as a designer. You can see from the illustrations below that Leonardo believed in the value of recording things. Drawing was a way in which he learnt to analyse things, both natural and man made. This is how he discovered many of nature's design secrets. An example of this is his drawing of the human body from observation only. He drew it in different layers and from different angles, all of which led him to discover a great deal about the science of

levers. He analysed birds and animals in a similar way, applying what he learnt to the design problems he was confronted with. This enabled him to design machines that, for the time, were well in advance of anything else. Another thing he has taught us is the importance of putting together all kinds of knowledge from all kinds of areas and looking at the whole aspect of the problem or object. This approach is particularly useful to you because your studies are becoming more and more like this.

Although there is much more knowledge in the world today than when Leonardo was working, we do have machines (computers) that help us deal with it. These computers enable us to bring all sorts of information together on any one subject. It is interesting to ponder how Leonardo da Vinci would have used this technology had it been available to him. Who knows what he would have designed with its help!

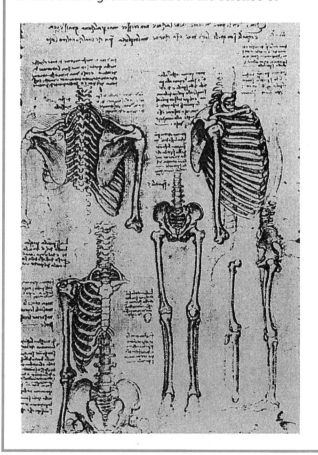

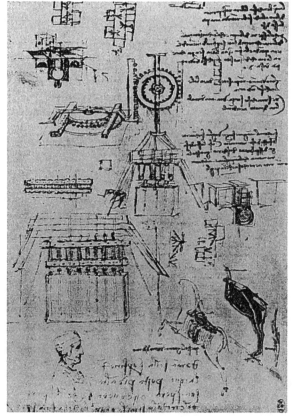

MARY QUANT

Moving closer to present times you find a second designer who proved to have great ability and who set new standards and trends.

Mary Quant was one of the first fashion designers to design and produce clothes specifically for the young. Until this time teenagers wore clothes which were either simply extensions of children's clothes and fashion or adult clothes made smaller. Mary's entry into the fashion world was marked by bright new colours and patterns. Another very successful trend she did much to establish was selling clothes through 'boutiques' rather than through conventional shops. It's rather difficult to understand now but in the 'sixties' the shopping public, once inside a shop, were not free to browse around but would be immediately confronted by a sales assistant!

In Mary's Chelsea boutique young people could browse through clothes while talking to their friends. This made the whole experience of shopping much more fun and resulted in Mary's boutique becoming a favourite meeting place. 'I had' she said, 'always wanted the young to have fashions of their own ... absolutely 20th century fashions ... but I knew nothing about the fashion business.'

Mary, however, soon set about learning how to design the clothes she wanted. Later on she learnt how to produce them herself. After this she went on to understand the manufacturing techniques. This meant that Mary could produce large amounts of fashionable clothes at reasonable prices. She did not start designing her clothes right from scratch, however. Instead she began by adapting and developing other people's designs. This is probably how you will begin your design process.

Like lots of other people with great ideas but little experience Mary made many mistakes. However, because she had lots of enthusiasm and believed in what she was doing Mary Quant established herself as a great leader in fashions for the young. Later on Mary went on to design underwear and make-up. Soon she had a business worth many millions of pounds and she was selling to hundreds of shops both in this country and abroad. In 1966 she received the OBE for her services to fashion exports and wore a mini skirt to Buckingham Palace to collect the award!

Designs by Mary Quant in the late fifties

L EVEL DESCRIPTIONS: DESIGNING

At the start of Key Stage 3 the majority of pupils will have reached at least Level 4 in Technology. By the end of Key Stage 3 most pupils should be within the range of Levels 4–7. Levels 5–6 are the target for 14-year-olds. Level 8 is the standard reached by very able pupils.

Use our checklist to assess the Level reached, by ticking the skills that have been mastered.

Level 4

☐ When designing and making, gather information independently, and use it to help generate a number of ideas.

☐ Recognize that users have views and preferences, and begin to take them into account.

☐ Evaluate work as it develops, bearing in mind the purposes for which it is intended.

☐ Illustrate alternatives using sketches and models and make choices between them, showing an awareness of constraints.

Level 5

☐ When designing and making, generate ideas that draw upon external sources and an understanding of the characteristics of familiar products.

☐ Clarify ideas through discussion, drawing and modelling, using knowledge and understanding of the appropriate programme of study to help.

☐ Evaluate ideas, showing understanding of the situations in which the designs will have to function, and an awareness of resources as a constraint.

Level 6

☐ When designing and making, generate ideas that draw on a wider range of sources of information, including those not immediately related to the task, and an understanding of the form and function of familiar products.

☐ Develop criteria for designs, which take into account appearance, function, safety, reliability and the users and purposes for which they are intended, and use these to formulate a design proposal.

☐ Make preliminary models to explore and test the design thinking, and use formal drawing methods to communicate intentions.

Level 7

☐ When designing and making, identify the appropriate sources of information and use them to help generate ideas.

☐ Investigate the characteristics of familiar products, including form, function and production processes, in order to develop ideas. Take into account the working characteristics of materials and components.

☐ Recognize the different needs of a variety of users, and use appropriate evaluation techniques to identify ways forward.

☐ Use knowledge and understanding of the Key Stage 3 Programme of Study to develop realistic intentions, communicated to others through a variety of media, to show how the designs will function in use.

Level 8

☐ When designing and making, use a range of strategies to help generate appropriate ideas.

☐ Identify how the needs and preferences of users are reflected in existing products, and relate these ideas to own work.

☐ Make decisions on materials and techniques, based on an understanding of their physical and working characteristics.

☐ Identify the conflicting demands on the designs, identify and communicate how design ideas address these demands, and use this analysis to produce a design proposal.

Exceptional performance

☐ When designing and making, systematically seek out information to aid design thinking, recognizing the needs of a variety of client groups.

☐ Draw on knowledge and understanding of the Key Stage 3 Programme of Study to arrive at a justifiable optimum solution through modelling, and communicate to others the key features of the designs, together with details that will aid manufacture.

Answers to Now test yourself

Photo-joiners on page 23
The balloon

1   Lines link the photographs together.

2 and 3   Two shapes re-occur constantly. One is the triangles that make up the balloon. A second shape that re-occurs in the machinery is that of a circle.

The school building

1   There are two things which help to create the feeling of depth in the picture. One is the gap between the photographer's feet and the rest of the picture. The other is the lines in between the concrete.

2 and 3   The parts of the picture that are of particular interest to the artist are the door and the bell tower. Your attention is drawn to them because they are repeated several times.

4   The order of importance is shape, pattern, line and texture.

Page 25 (box 1)

(a) Red

(b) Green

(c) Yellow

Page 25 (box 2)

In order to wire a 13 amp plug correctly you need to know that:

– the green and yellow wire goes to the EARTH terminal
– the brown wire goes to the LIVE terminal
– the blue wire goes to the NEUTRAL terminal

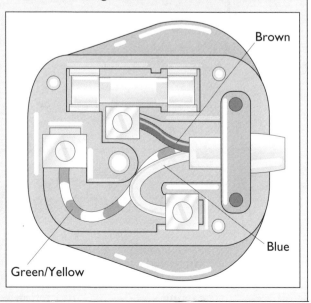

Brown

Blue

Green/Yellow

CHAPTER 2

*M*aking

I NTRODUCTION

In technology you will be working with a variety of materials such as paper, fabrics, wood, metal and plastic. The choice of material will depend upon what properties are required for a specific situation.

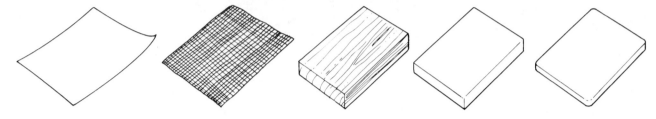

C HOICE OF MATERIAL

It is not easy to select which material is best for a design activity. To make successful choices you need to know and understand the materials, as well as having worked with them. The final choice is often a compromise because several factors have to be considered. These include:

1 THE TASK

In order to perform a task, a material may need to combine several important qualities – colour, weight, hardness, rigidity, smoothness, flexibility, texture.

The young technologist at work

Consider the sketches below and decide which of the qualities outlined above are needed in each case, and which sort of material has been chosen.

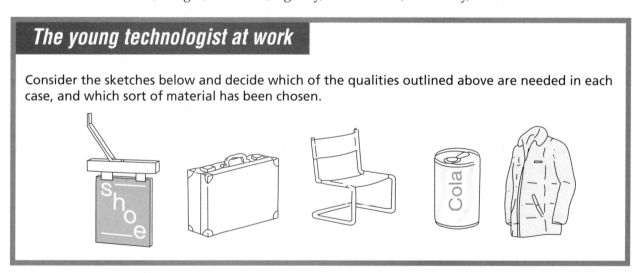

---

2 THE SCALE OF PRODUCTION

The material chosen should be related to the number of items you intend to make. Large-scale production often requires cheaper and more 'easy to work with' materials than one-off creations, made by craftsmen. In the exercises which you do, you will be using small-scale production methods.

The young technologist at work

With this in mind, look at the illustrations below. These show the contrast between a fibreglass catamaran and a balsa wood model. Take a while to think about the properties of the materials for these two items.

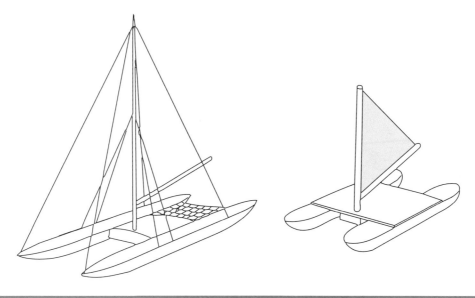

3 THE COST

When thinking about costs, do not just consider the capital cost of buying the material. You also need to take account of the time taken to work the material into shape and any processing needed, for example, joining it to other components and giving it a finish. The amount of waste may also be important. Sometimes expensive materials are best to use because many of them have little wastage and so are the cheapest to work with! The quality of the artefact needed may determine the choice of material used.

The young technologist at work

Think about the cost of the material used for the various forms of underwear shown below.

4 THE AVAILABLE MATERIAL

From your point of view you will be interested in using low-cost materials because you are doing only experimental exercises. So, off-cuts are the order of the day! Usually, however, materials are bought in standard sizes and to particular specifications. Different materials come in different forms, e.g. rolls, pellets, sheets, square bars, etc.

The sketches below show several waste products which you could put to good use in some of the assignments that follow.

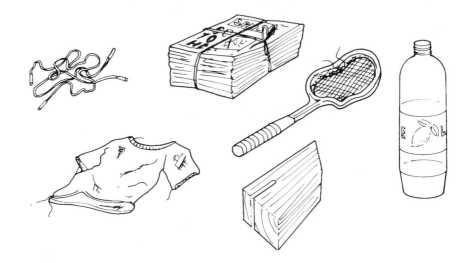

5 THE PROPERTIES OF MATERIALS

Each material has particular qualities which make it unique. It is thus more suitable for some situations rather than others. For example, in general, materials used in construction, like steel, must be hard and strong whereas materials used in fashion often need to be soft and colourful, e.g. silk or cotton.

However, even when a material like wood is looked at, it can be seen that there are many different types and each has varying properties.

The properties of materials can be classified into two types:

(a) Mechanical

As you are involved in making things from materials you need to know what impact can be withstood before the material changes in any way. Various tests have been applied to determine the effect of different forces and shocks on materials and components.

Such tests can reveal the following properties:

STRENGTH: the ability to withstand force without breaking. For example, you might wish to use *steel wire* instead of string.

ELASTICITY: the ability to stretch and bend when subject to loads and then regain their normal shape, e.g. *elastic band*

HARDNESS: the ability to resist abrasive wear and attempts to deform the material, e.g. *carbon fibre drill bit*

TOUGHNESS: the ability to withstand big shocks, e.g. *copper wires*

BRITTLENESS: the tendency to tolerate only a little strain before fracturing, e.g. *glass*

DURABILITY: the ability to withstand wear and tear and corrosion, e.g. *PVC window frames*

STABILITY: the ability to resist changing in size and shape, e.g. *melamine table top*. Such changes can be caused by different temperatures and amounts of moisture (e.g. wood may warp).

PLASTICITY: the ability to change shape permanently without breaking, e.g. *clay*

DUCTILITY: the ability to change shape easily, e.g. *rubber*

CONDUCTIVITY: the ability to let heat pass through, e.g. *metal radiator*

(b) Physical

Materials also have distinctive physical differences. These can be modified or changed in order to meet certain aims. For example, wood is often stained to achieve a particular finish.

The main physical properties are:

COLOUR: this can be natural or artificial

ODOUR: some materials give out a smell, e.g. pine trees

OPTICAL: this is the extent to which you can see through something. For example, a glass dish is transparent whereas a wooden pencil is opaque.

THERMAL: the reaction to heat varies between materials. For example, copper conducts heat well and thus becomes hot, whereas foam traps air and so insulates.

ELECTRICAL: this shows the resistance to a flow of current. For example, glass is a good insulator against electricity, whereas copper is a good conductor.

FUSIBILITY: this is the ability to change from a solid into a liquid if heated, e.g. metal at various temperatures

Properties of metals

There are three types of metal:

FERROUS: iron based with additions of other substances, e.g. steel. Ferrous metals rust and will be attracted to a magnet.

NON-FERROUS: do not contain iron, e.g. copper, aluminium, lead, tin. These do not rust and are not attracted to magnets.

ALLOYS: metals which are a mixture of at least two other metals. This is done to achieve certain desirable qualities. For example:
stainless steel is a ferrous alloy of steel and chromium
brass is a non-ferrous alloy of copper and zinc

The table below gives a summary of the main metals, their properties and uses. There are many varieties within each metal named. For example, types of steel include mild steel which is easy to use compared to high carbon steel which is difficult to cut.

Name	Type	Uses	Main properties
Cast iron	ferrous	brake disc, vice	hard skin (but brittle core), strong, doesn't bend
Steel	ferrous	many tools	strong (but corrodes), malleable, easy to join
Copper	non-ferrous	electrical wires	good conductor, tough, malleable, solders well (but expensive)
Lead	non-ferrous	roof covering	soft (but weak), heavy, malleable, does not corrode
Stainless steel	alloy	cutlery	hard, corrosion resistant, difficult to cut, tough

Properties of wood

Timber is classified by the type of tree from which it comes. There are three categories:

SOFTWOODS: trees with needle-like leaves, e.g. pine and spruce

HARDWOODS: trees with broad leaves, e.g. mahogany and oak

MANUFACTURED BOARDS: hardwood and softwood can be combined to produce materials such as plywood and chipboard. These have multiple uses and come in many varieties. For example, veneered chipboard (conti-board) is more expensive than standard particle board but has a better finish.

Man made boards are increasingly used because they can be manufactured to create a variety of qualities that suit specific needs. For example, medium density fibre board (MDF) is dense and heavy, unaffected by changes in humidity and an electrical insulator unlike other composite boards. MDF seems to have some characteristics of solid timber, e.g. strength, resistance to water and is capable of being shaped. It can be fashioned with traditional hand tools such as planes and chisels. In addition, many finishes can be easily applied to it.

The table below shows the main timbers, their properties and their uses. Again the list is selective, rather than complete, as woods such as elm, beech, teak and cedar have been ignored.

Name	Type	Uses	Main properties
Scots pine	soft	construction	easy to paint and work, strong, cheap
Spruce	soft	furniture	strong but not durable, small hard knots
Mahogany	hard	furniture, veneers	strong, durable, easy to work but can warp
Oak	hard	boats, fence posts	very strong and durable, hard, expensive
Chipboard	manufactured	shelves, work tops	strong, large flat sheets, various types
Ash	hard	car bodies, caravans	strong, springy

Properties of plastics

There are two main groups of plastics:

THERMOPLASTICS: soften when heated and lose rigidity at + 100°C. They are easily moulded and harden when they cool. There are many types, e.g. PVC (polyvinyl chloride).

THERMOSETS: can withstand high temperatures and thus retain their form. They are also good thermal insulators, e.g. polyester resin, melamine.

The table on the next page shows the main plastics, their uses and their working characteristics. Polystyrene comes in several forms and the table refers to the conventional form. However, it can be specially toughened or produced in a foam form, as used in packaging and insulation tiles.

In recent years, *additives* have been applied to plastics to improve their mechanical properties. There are many different types and uses of additives. For example, adding asbestos improves resistance to temperature. Similarly, *lamination* and *bonding* with resin can help to strengthen thermosetting plastics. Paper cloth and other cheap materials impregnated with melamine resin can produce Formica, often used on work surfaces.

Name	Type	Uses	Properties
Polythene	thermoplastic	carrier bags, squeezy bottles	tough, flexible, various colours, cheap
Polystyrene	thermoplastic	disposable cutlery, model kits	light but little strength, resists water, transparent
Melamine	thermoset	buttons, kitchen work surfaces	strong, various colours, odourless, scratch and stain resistant
Urea formaldehyde	thermoset	adhesives, fittings, appliance parts	hard and strong, heat resistant, various colours, good insulator

Changing the properties of materials

Materials are often combined and changed in order to create certain performance characteristics. *Heating* metal and plastic is one way to change their nature. However, at Key Stage 3 it is unlikely that you will perform such operations. Therefore, heat treatment will just be introduced here.

Metals can be hardened, tempered and annealed. These are done at very high temperatures. Material once softened can be bent in an anvil.

Plastics can be softened by heat and then deformed. There are several possible methods – wire bending, vacuum forming and blow moulding. Bending jigs will hold the thermoplastic sheets in the required position until they cool.

Timber can also be formed by bending it in one direction. Complicated patterns can be created. Brackets are usually needed to give the shape, as the timber strips are glued and clamped between two flexible steel strips.

As wood can warp if subject to moisture, this can be used to shape it. Soaking timber in water, or subjecting it to steam, will help it bend to the desired shape. Some timbers bend more easily than others. The famous longbow won many battles for the English because it was made from *yew* which gave it special strength. If the bows had been made from *oak*, which has strength but no 'give', they would have been less effective weapons.

Materials can also be reformed by *pressing* and *casting*. When heated, metals will melt. The liquid metal can then be poured into a mould so that the desired form can be held until the metal becomes set. There is considerable skill in mould making, particularly in ensuring that the cast is withdrawn easily from the pattern. Presses can exert a lot of pressure and thus enable changes to be made in the shape of metal.

Punches and dies work together in *shearing* metal. They are made from hardened high-carbon chromium alloy steel and keep a sharp edge. Punches and dies can also be used to bend metals. A good example of this is their use to insert eyelets in tents and shoes. A metal eyelet is 'crimped' around the canvas or leather to help spread the load. This prevents the guy ropes rubbing and tearing the material of the tent.

6 TOOLS AND EQUIPMENT

After designing has taken place and before making can begin, several other processes need to be carried out. These require basic tools and equipment. The processes are MARKING OUT, MEASUREMENT and HOLDING. The tools to be used will vary with the type of material used. Usually we are working with **TIMBER, METAL, PLASTIC** or **FABRIC**. For the processes described below, common examples of the tools to be used are given. There will of course be other possible tools that could be used.

Marking out

This should be done very carefully and accurately to avoid wasting time and materials.

LINES
Timber:	marking knife and try square
Metal:	scriber (this has a hardened steel point for scratching the surface)
Plastic:	felt-tipped pen
Fabric:	pencil and chalk

PARALLEL LINES A mortise gauge should be used.

HOLES and CIRCLES Marking a hole for a drill can be done with a centre punch and a heavy hammer. If circles are needed then a pair of compasses should be used on wood and cloth. Spring dividers can be used to scratch circles on metal and acrylic surfaces. Small circles can be marked out with a compass. Large circles can be marked out with a length of string and a securing device such as a stake.

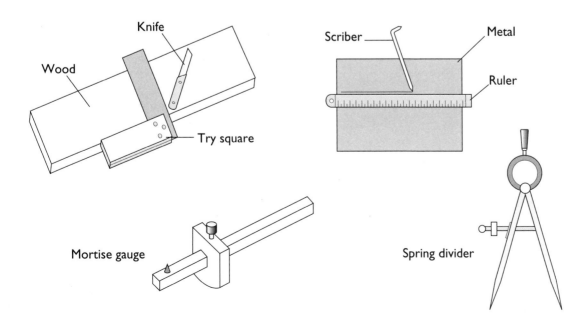

Knife — Wood — Try square

Scriber — Metal — Ruler

Mortise gauge

Spring divider

Now test yourself

1 How could you mark out the circles on a football pitch?

2 How would you mark out an oval or an ellipse?

Answers on p. 78

Measurement

The choice of measuring device does not vary with the material used, as in the marking out process. It depends rather on the degree of accuracy needed.

In most cases when working with resistant materials a *steel rule* (150 mm) is appropriate, as it gives precision and is easy to use. For greater lengths an extendible steel tape should be used.

When working with wool or cloth, *a dressmaker's tape measure* should be used. This is useful for measuring wrist and hip sizes.

If a scale needs subdividing very accurately into smaller parts, you could use *callipers*. They can be used on all types of material.

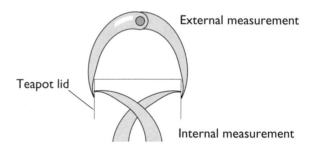

Holding

There are many holding devices to help with most processes from the marking out stage through to finishing. The devices vary from hands and hand-held equipment, such as pliers, to heavy benches. Dressmaker's pins are a very simple and effective means of holding fabrics together.

Now test yourself

3 Look around the kitchen and see what holding utensils you can find.

The choice of holding device depends on the type of material being used, the amount of movement which can be allowed or is needed, and whether the material is hot or cold.

Clamps

These are used mainly for small-scale work. There are many types but the two most common are the G clamp for up to 300 mm and the sash clamp for up to 2000 mm. Other equipment for clamping small pieces of materials include pliers and wrenches. The latter lock onto the material strongly.

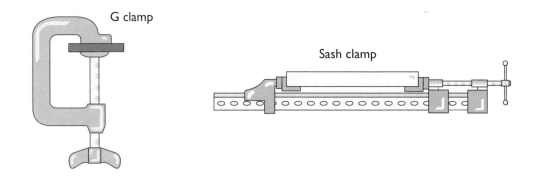

G clamp

Sash clamp

Vices

These are more versatile than clamps. They are often secured to work benches, so vices can be used to hold long and broad materials, as well as short and thin ones.

The vice enables timber to be held stable for planing, sawing and drilling. Sheet metal can be bent in a vice also.

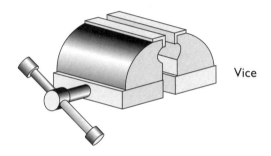

Vice

Tongs

Sometimes materials are hot from the heating process and so they need to be picked up safely or held in the appropriate place. The illustration shows close-mouth tongs for thin materials but there are several other types.

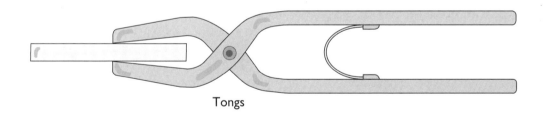

Tongs

Now test yourself

4 How many examples of these devices can you find in the house?

5 Can you think of holding devices, which are not clamps, vices and tongs, found in the house?

Answers on p. 78

51

B ASIC TOOLS

In this section we consider the main general uses of each tool. Later we will outline their role in shaping and forming materials and in assembly work.

Saws

There are a large variety of saws which can be used. The one chosen depends upon the material and the intricacy of the cutting. For example, saws designed for timber are often not hard enough to cut metal, whereas metalworking saws may cut wood but rather inefficiently. There are also special saws for cutting meat and bread.

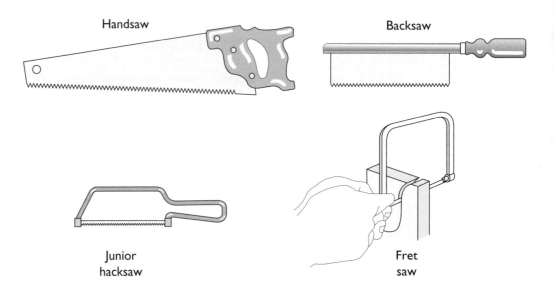

Handsaw   Backsaw

Junior hacksaw   Fret saw

Handsaws are used for large pieces of wood. There are rip saws (which cut along the grain) and cross cut saws (which cut across the grain). They are usually 650 mm long with teeth every 5 mm (4 mm on cross cut saws which have finer teeth). Rip saws have teeth like chisels whereas cross cut saws have teeth sharpened like knife points.

Backsaws are used for wood and plastic where intricate work is needed. The tenon saw is typical with a blade about 250 mm long and teeth every 2 mm.

Hacksaws are used for metal and plastic work. They vary in size according to the heaviness of the job. There are two-handed saws for jobs for which the junior hacksaw is too flimsy. Blades are replaceable and their teeth differ. Thus fine blades are needed for hard materials and coarse blades are used on soft materials. Significantly, the blade can be turned through 90°.

Fretsaws So far we have been considering sawing in straight lines. However, sometimes curves need to be sawn. In this case a *coping saw* is used for wood and plastic, whilst a *piercing saw* would be used for metal, silversmithing and other fine work because of its thin blade.

Special saws These are made for specific jobs. Two examples are keyhole saws and floorboard saws.

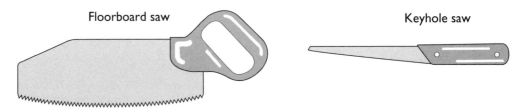

Floorboard saw   Keyhole saw

Machine saws Adjustable blades can be used with these powerful tools, which are useful with all materials. However, they are only used by suitably qualified adults because of the danger involved.

Planes

Planes carve and scrape off a thin layer of material as they are pushed along. They are set at a specific angle and devised to direct the waste material away.

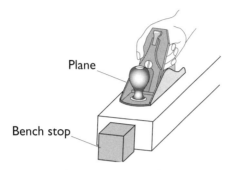

Wood planes The two most frequently used are:

Jack planes – 400 mm long and used for general planing.

Smoothing planes – 250 mm long, lighter and used more for finishing or planing the grain.

Most planes are *adjustable.* The height of the blade and the angle of the blade can be changed. There are also numerous special purpose planes for specific operations, e.g. rebate planes to cut grooves and spokeshaves for working on curved surfaces.

Paper planes Bookbinders use several types of paper plane to assemble books.

Kitchen planes Potato peelers and butter curlers are examples of these.

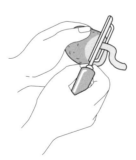

Drills and other hole makers

The simplest type of hole maker is a spike. These can be used with many different materials. In the kitchen, we would call a spike a skewer and use it in a variety of ways.

Now test yourself

6 What would you use a skewer for?   Answer on p. 78

A more sophisticated hole maker is an apple corer. This device is used in a twisting motion and is similar to a drill as it rotates when pressed in contact with the fruit.

Drills are needed to make holes in wood, metal and plastic. Twist drills are the most commonly used and, fitted with tungsten carbide tips, will drill most materials effectively.

Before using a drill it is helpful to start holes with a *bradawl.* Hand drills are either *wheel braces* (8 mm drill) or *breast drills* (up to 12 mm in size).

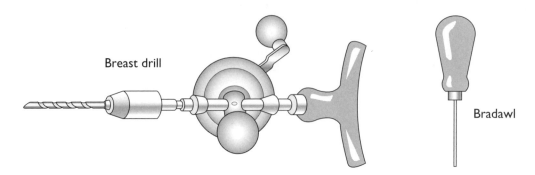

Breast drill

Bradawl

Portable drills which are electrically or battery powered are becoming increasingly popular. Usually they are single speed but they contain a variety of bits for use with different materials and working in various sizes.

Chisels

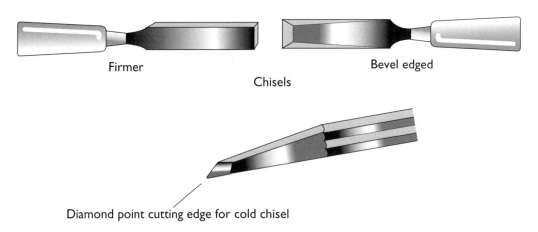

Firmer

Chisels

Bevel edged

Diamond point cutting edge for cold chisel

These are used only with metal and wood, not plastic.

Firmer chisels are used for general bench work in wood. They have a square edged blade and vary in width from 3 mm to 50 mm. For heavy work a *mortise chisel* with thick blades would be used.

Bevel edged chisels are also used for wood, but for light work and getting into corners.

Cold chisels are used to fashion metal so they need hardened and tempered cutting edges. The cutting edges can be flat, cross cut, diamond point or round nosed, depending on how the metal has to be cut.

Scrapers are used in a similar way to chisels to shape materials, often to give a fine finish.

Files, rasps and graters

Files are used for shaping. They remove material by a rubbing action. There are many types, classified according to types and frequency of teeth. For most general work a hand file would be used. These are flat, parallel and have one safe uncut edge. Usually they are made of high carbon steel and can be used on wood, plastic and metal.

Hand file

A rasp is a very coarse file which removes material in the same way as a food grater. However, with food graters it is the material that is removed which is required.

Hammers and mallets

The general function of these tools is fairly obvious but hammers also have other uses. For example, claw hammers can be used to extract nails, as well as knock them in. There are also many special purpose hammers, particularly for use with metal to secure fine finishes. A shrinking hammer is used in car body repair and a steak hammer for tenderizing meat.

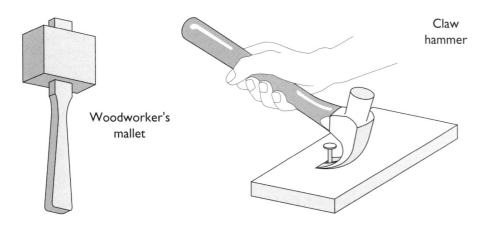

Claw hammer

Woodworker's mallet

Similarly with mallets there are specialist tools for both wood and metal. For example, a woodworker's mallet would be used for striking a chisel when shaping wood.

Screwdrivers

These are used primarily in the assembly process. They should be carefully matched to the size and shape of the screw slot.

The traditional slot screwdriver most commonly used for general purpose work is the *cabinet screwdriver.* It has a round blade and varies in size from 75 mm to 300 mm long. Electricians use insulated blades to avoid electrocution.

The more modern type is the *Phillips screwdriver* which has a cross head. These have become much more common partly because they are easier for robots to handle.

Crosshead   Slot

7 SHAPING AND FORMING MATERIALS

There are many methods of shaping and forming materials and most create wastage.

Cutting

This involves a sharpened edge. A craft knife (on a cutting board) is a good example. A more unusual example would be a 'quick-unpick' when it is used to unpick fabric seams by cutting through stitches.

Shearing

This involves two cutting edges coming together, e.g. a pair of scissors. Tin snips are used to cut metal sheet. Most fabrics can be cut with scissors but to prevent the edges from fraying, pinking shears are used to create a crinkle cut (crimped) edge. Because the threads are different lengths they do not fall away so easily.

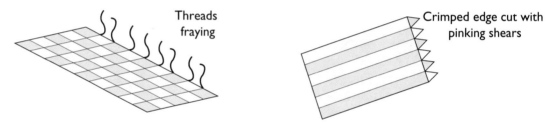

Sawing

Assuming that you have measured and marked your piece of work, when sawing you should always cut to the waste side of the line. This will allow a small margin for error and an amount for finishing, perhaps with a plane if it is a wooden piece.

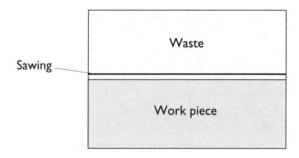

The choice of saw will depend on the material to be cut (see earlier). Selecting the correct blade is important. For example, soft materials require a coarse pitch and hard materials need a fine pitch. Usually, it is wise to use the free hand to grip the work piece or the bench if the wood is in a vice.

Planing

You need to check that planes are correctly set and sharp before work commences. To plane, press firmly at the front as you start and push from the back; then release as the plane clears the work. If shavings jam, then remove them carefully with your fingers.

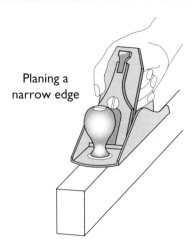

Planing a
narrow edge

When planing along a narrow edge you need to stop the plane wobbling. To steady the plane, hold the toe rather than the knob but keep your fingers well away from the blade.

Filing

Files should always be used with handles. You use both hands normally for filing. There are two types of filing:

Cross filing – to remove and shape material by running the file across the material.

Draw filing – to give improved surface finish by running the file up and down the piece.

Usually with filing, your thumb should be at the top of the handle for guidance. It is a good idea to place material in a vice at a comfortable height. As files only cut on the forward stroke, try to use the whole length of the file and downward pressure. For draw filing a smoother file is needed. An even better finish can be obtained by wrapping a piece of emery cloth around the file.

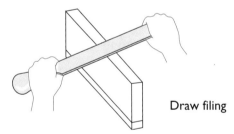

Draw filing

Chiselling

There are two types of chiselling:

Paring – using a bevel edged chisel to remove *small* shavings with hand pressure. One hand holds the handle whilst the other guides the cutting edge.

Chopping – using a mortise chisel to remove *large* chips by applying a hammer or mallet to the handle. One hand is on the chisel, the other hand on the mallet.

In both cases great care should be taken. In the case of paring ensure that both hands are behind the cutting edge, i.e. chisel away from your body. When chopping make sure that the work is clamped down and the chisel is firmly held. Do not use a hammer on a wooden handled chisel as it will cause damage. Always keep chisels sharp.

Although most chiselling is done on wood, the technique can be applied to metal. Cold chisels work vertically with the metal being supported on a soft steel cutting block.

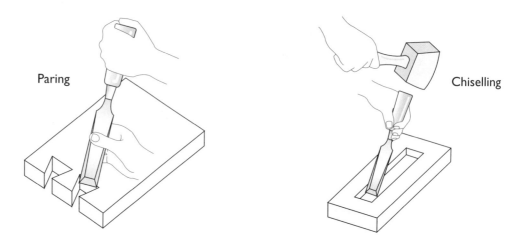

Paring

Chiselling

Drilling

Certain steps need to be taken when drilling. The centre of the hole should be very clearly marked to reduce error, because once a hole is drilled it remains there. The work to be drilled should be securely clamped in place.

When boring through wood the bit should first pierce through and then be removed. The hole can then be completed from the reverse side. This gives a clean hole and reduces the likelihood of splitting the wood.

Pillar drills, which are floor or bench located, enable drilling to be done at different speeds. The drill speed needed depends on the material and the diameter of the drill. For example, acrylic requires a faster speed than mild steel. Larger diameter drills necessitate a lower drill speed, irrespective of the material.

With metal and plastic, when a power drill breaks through there is a danger that it will 'snatch' or become locked together with the material. This can be dangerous because the drill may tear the material from its mounting. You should immediately reduce the downward pressure.

8 JOINING AND COMBINING MATERIALS

Most projects require materials to be joined together. This can be done either permanently or temporarily. However, some materials are *compliant* (they can be combined without much resistance) whereas others are *resistant* (they require force to change their shape and form). This is further complicated by the fact that some materials can be either compliant or resistant, depending on their state. For example, wet clay is soft and pliable but once it is fired it becomes resistant.

T EMPORARY FIXING

The easiest way to join some materials together in the short term is by using pins and tacks, e.g. in dressmaking. Blu-Tack is very useful for temporary fixing, as is masking tape.

Resistant materials can be joined temporarily with certain glues, e.g. PVA (polyvinyl acetate), a white glue (not woodworking adhesive) which can be washed off afterwards. The strongest temporary fixings are those that make use of screw threads, nuts and bolts. The virtue is that assembling things in this way enables the finished article to be disassembled if necessary.

PERMANENT JOINING

For permanent joints that cannot be dismantled various methods are used. Simple wood joints are usually glued and may be screwed as well for strength. Joining metal is done with rivets, adhesives or a heat process. This latter could be soldering, welding or brazing.

Adhesives

Most adhesives are in liquid form. There are four main *groups* of adhesives:

- Natural – made from naturally occurring plants or animals
- Thermoplastics – made from one synthetic glue, and easily applied
- Thermosets – made by combining liquids or powders to produce a bonding which sets hard and is very strong
- Elastomers – made from synthetic rubber and commonly called 'contact adhesive'

Correct selection of the adhesive to use is crucial. The table below gives the basic information required for the four main types of adhesive. The epoxy type which uses resin and hardener mixed requires clamping, whilst the other three types listed need only light pressure.

	Type of adhesive	Example	Setting time	Strength	Water resistance	Other properties
A	latex	Copydex	15–30 min.	good	good	cheap, non-toxic
B	cements	Polystyrene	1–3 hours	fair	fair	use with kits
C	epoxy	Araldite	20–60 min.	excellent	excellent	requires clamping, expensive
D	contact	Evostick	instant	good	good	use in well-ventilated area

The second table shows which types of adhesive should be used when bonding materials together. So, for example, if you are combining two pieces of plastic you should use a cement (B) or a contact adhesive (D) for the best results.

Bonding materials together				
	TIMBER	METAL	PLASTIC	TEXTILES
TIMBER	D	ACD	ABD	AD
METAL	ACD	ABD	AD	AD
PLASTIC	BD	AD	BD	AD
TEXTILES	AD	ACD	AD	AD

Useful tips when gluing

ALWAYS READ THE INSTRUCTIONS.

* Clean any dust, dirt, oil or moisture off the surfaces to be glued.
* Have a dry run at assembly, if appropriate, so that you can check the need for clamps, etc.
* Make sure there is a cloth handy for the removal of any excess which is applied accidentally.
* Read the instructions about the glue carefully. For example, with contact adhesives you often need plenty of ventilation.
* When applying glue avoid getting it on your fingers.
* Clean away any unwanted glue before it sets.
* Do not apply any form of finish to the surfaces to be glued.

WOOD JOINTS

There are many types of joints to choose from when combining pieces of wood, ranging from the simple to the complicated. An important factor in choosing is the amount of *load* which the joint needs to bear. Generally, screwed joints are stronger than nailed ones.

Butt and mitre joints

These are simple but weak joints, as only a small area is glued. They can be strengthened with nails. A picture frame is an example of the butt joint.

On the inside strengthening can be applied with *battens.* The battens can be glued and screwed.

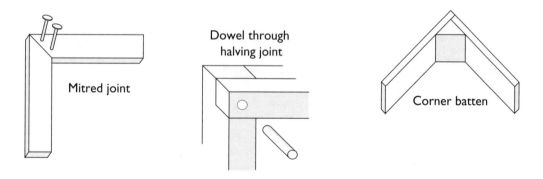

Mitred joint

Dowel through halving joint

Corner batten

Another means of strengthening these joints is by use of a *dowel,* which can go through holes inserted in each piece. In the illustration the joint has been halved. This means that half of the thickness of the wood at the joint has been removed. Dowels are glued into the holes to add further strength.

Bridle joints

These are stronger than butt and mitre joints. They can be used at corners or for 'T' joints. In addition they can be pegged with a dowel. They are often used in making light frames, as they are more decorative than halving joints.

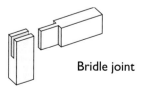

Bridle joint

Mortise and tenon joints

These joints are stronger than bridle joints. They are a form of 'T' joint, and can either go through the piece or be closed at one end. The name derives from the fact that the wood is normally cut with a tenon saw and a mortise chisel. The joint is glued and wedged in place.

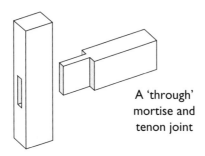

A 'through' mortise and tenon joint

Dovetail joints

These are the strongest box corner joints and can look attractive. However, they are difficult to construct and need careful cutting out. The dovetail on each part has a pin and a tail, with the protruding pin approximately half the width of the adjacent tail. Each side pin should be wider to give extra strength.

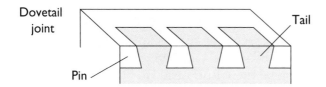

Dovetail joint

Tail

Pin

Dovetail joints can only be assembled in one direction and can therefore only be pulled apart in one direction. Lapped dovetail joints are often used on drawer fronts.

The *comb* joint works in a similar principle to the dovetail. However, its pins and tails are rectangular and so they are easier to make. Like the dovetail, it gains strength from the creation of a large gluing area.

As solid timber is not used in anything like the quantity that it was, wood joints are becoming a thing of the past. Modern furniture is held together with *jointing blocks* and *steel plates,* whereas years ago each part of such furniture would require a special joint which would be cut by hand with great skill. Old tables and drawer chests are interesting to examine for all the different types of joint that can be found. Wooden doors and window frames still require joints.

Some of the most complex wood joints are to be found in roof structures, particularly barns where large timbers have to take and transmit great loads.

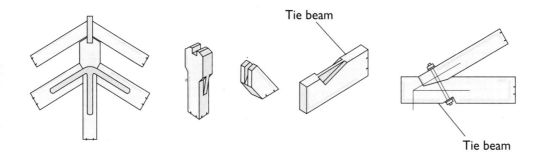

Tie beam

Tie beam

Chipboard

Chipboard is a composite made from sawdust and chippings, which means that it is environmentally friendly and relatively cheap. Since it is made by compression under great loads, it is very hard and can withstand a lot of pressure. However, because it has no structure (grain) it has little strength and so traditional wood joints cannot be used to join the materials together. Instead jointing blocks and other devices are needed. If you look at a modern kitchen you will see the use made of chipboard and its need for *specialist screws, hinges* and *fastenings.*

A further problem with chipboard is that, if it is not treated, it has little resistance to water. When damp, chipboard swells and sags and it can turn eventually to a pulp.

METAL JOINTS

These are permanent, unlike many wood joints. In soldering and welding heat is used to achieve the joints. Rivets can also be used with sheet metal to effect a permanent joint. The decision on which method to use for metal jointing depends on the metal, the stress to which the joint will be subjected and the structure of the work.

Soft solder

This is an alloy of tin and lead. It melts at + 185°C. As a jointing method it is easy and quick, particularly for brass, copper and metal sheet. The proportions of tin and lead in the solder should be varied with the task and metals involved. For example, if jointing sheet metal more lead needs to be used. This is because it melts at a higher temperature and so sets much harder. Conversely, if using solder for electronics more tin is required in the mix.

In order to apply the solder you use a soldering bit, which is *heated* by either a gas flame or an electric soldering iron. First you need to ensure that the surfaces are thoroughly *clean.* This can be done with steel wire wool or emery cloth. *Flux* is also required. This can be liquid, powder or paste and it is applied to the joint to keep the metal clean whilst it is being soldered. When soldering, the iron should be regularly dipped into the flux whilst it is hot then coated with solder. There are several ways to solder. For example, for difficult joints 'sweat' soldering is the best method. You need to coat both sides of the joint with a layer of solder then bring them together, heating carefully with a low flame whilst the joint is held firmly in place.

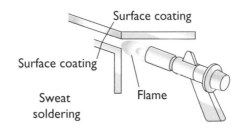

Surface coating

Surface coating

Sweat
soldering

Flame

Hard solder

This is similar to soft solder but involves much higher temperatures, typically + 650°C. The result is a stronger joint. There are two types of hard solder:

* *Brazing* – hardest solder with very high melting point (about 815°C), using an alloy of copper and zinc.
* *Silver* – hard solder with high temperatures (650–800°C), using an alloy of silver, copper and zinc.

In both cases joints need to be held securely, often with wire. Also, at these temperatures it is wise to surround the work with fire bricks. These will reflect the heat and maintain an even temperature. An oxy-acetylene welding torch will be used to provide the heat. The flame needs to be bushy rather than narrow so that the flux is not blown away from the joint.

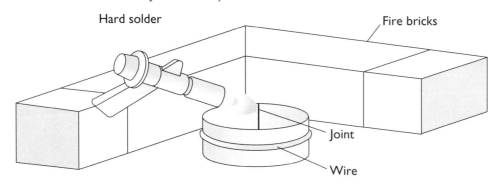

Welding

Although you will not be allowed to weld things, you need to know something about the usefulness of welding. Welding is the act of fusing together two pieces of metal into one piece. It is done under very high temperatures using oxy-acetylene *gas* equipment or *electric* arc welding equipment. Much protective shielding is needed, particularly over the eyes.

When welding, a pool of molten metal is created by the flame and a filler rod is continually dipped into it. The filler rod is the same metal as those being joined and it melts into the joint, thereby filling it and fusing the metal together. In electric arc welding the filler rod is flux coated.

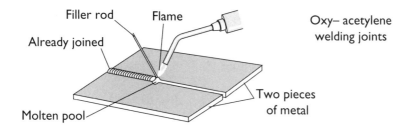

Riveting

Rivets can be used to join metal permanently. They do not require heat and so are classed as a 'cold jointing system'. Rivets are usually made of mild steel, copper or aluminium.

In 1872 a famous American who cut up wagon train canvas to make trousers decided that the best way to strengthen the canvas was to rivet it. His name was Jean Levi.

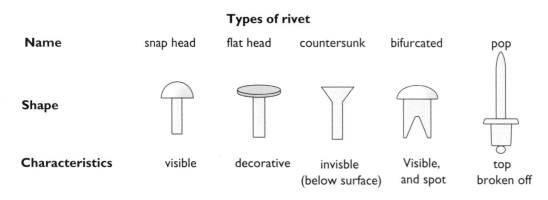

Types of rivet

Name	snap head	flat head	countersunk	bifurcated	pop
Shape					
Characteristics	visible	decorative	invisble (below surface)	Visible, and spot	top broken off

Before riveting a hole should be drilled in one of the pieces of metal. The second piece of metal should then be lined up and the rivet drilled. You need an engineer's hammer and a rivet set. The latter is used to tighten the joint, whilst the former swells the rivet to fill the drilled hole. The ball pen end of the hammer is then used to shape the rivet.

Generally the amount of rivet head above the surface should be 1½ times its diameter. The rivet head should be held on a snap in a vice. When access to both sides of a joint is not possible, pop rivets are used. These tend to be weaker but are quicker to fix.

Rivets can also be used with some types of wood, such as plywood, and with acrylic.

P LASTIC JOINTS

Plastic joints can be formed in several ways:

• Welding – using hot air torch (similar to metal joints)
• Gluing – using adhesive (similar to wood joints)
• Threading – using taps and dies

The most common means of joining plastic is by adhesive with a solvent or a cement.

Tips for gluing plastics

• Surfaces should be clean and free from moisture.
• Allow gaps with 'L', 'T' and butt joints.
• With solvents use masking tape to protect surrounding surface (and read manufacturer's instructions carefully).
• Assemble in well-ventilated space.
• Assemble joint quickly after adhesive has been applied.
• Lightly clamp (or firmly hold) joint until cement sets.
• Trim off excess glue with scalpel.
• Remove masking tape once adhesive is set hard.
• Polish any exposed cement much later.

Threading

The holes for joining two pieces of plastic (or wood) need to be drilled and tapped. Tapping is the cutting of the thread. This is done with a *die* on plastic (and metal). The size of the thread is marked on the die. There are three sorts of tap – *taper, second and plug,* which should be used in sequence. Each is made of high speed steel.

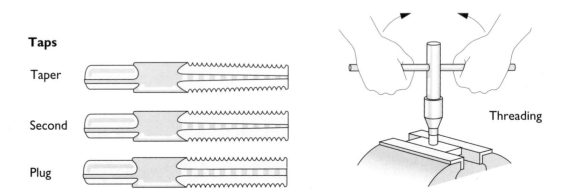

Taps

Taper

Second

Plug

Threading

You should drill a pilot hole to start, then apply lubricant or paste. With the die holder, cut clockwise for a half turn, using the taper tap first. Then release the scurf with a quarter turn anti-clockwise. The process is then continued with the second tap which has a shorter taper. This is followed by the plug tap which has a chamfered end. Care should be taken with the taps because they are brittle. This is particularly important with blind holes where you do not drill through the plastic.

F ABRIC JOINING

Fabrics are usually compliant and can be joined in several ways by stitches, zips, buttons, press-studs and seams.

The three most common types of seam are:

• Flat seam
• French seam
• Lap and fell seam

9 FINISHING

The surface of a material can be enhanced by the finish and the texture. A surface FINISH performs several functions:

• It can improve the working of the object, e.g. wax on furniture.
• It may protect the object, e.g. polyurethane finish to keep water out, creosote to prevent wood decay.
• It can make the object more attractive, e.g. paint of different colours.

Closely linked with finish is the TEXTURE of an object. Texture gives 'feel' and enables the surface to have different qualities. For example, a texture could be rough or smooth, making the surface feel warm or cold. Furthermore, the texture could give visual interest by the contrast between different patterns. Some texture which occurs naturally is random, whereas artificial texture can be regular.

Textures can perform the same functions as finishes. A coarse texture might create a better grip and it could hide scratches and other errors. Similarly, contrasting textures on an item such as a briefcase may enhance the appearance and add decoration. In addition, some synthetic textures can be used to suggest that more expensive materials have been used in production, e.g. silver plating.

Fillers

Just before finishing, you may need to conceal surface blemishes. These can arise from errors, faulty workmanship or poor quality materials. In addition you may want to hide a joint or just make a surface smooth.

There are wood fillers in a range of colours, polyesters which will bond metal, and various waterproofing fillers. They can be applied with tools of different dexterity, ranging from spatulas for small areas to large knives for bigger surfaces.

Finishing is not always carried out only at the end of a project or production. Sometimes a component can be finished before it is joined with something else. This may be done to make the task easier to accomplish, e.g. drawers inside a cabinet.

Before applying any finish or texture it is advisable to experiment on a piece of scrap material. Having decided on the finish, then practise doing it before making the final application because repeating the skill will often make your finish much better.

Gloss and matt finishes

Gloss finishes are highly polished and make the main features stand out, but they show up marks and dust. Matt finishes will be dull and attract less attention. However, because they do not show marks and fingerprints they need less cleaning!

F INISHING WOOD

Generally the first part of the finishing process for wood is *planing*. This is usually followed by cleaning up with *abrasive* paper (popularly called sandpaper). This enables you to achieve a high quality finish. There are different grades of abrasive paper, from coarse to fine. Abrasive paper should be wrapped tightly around a cork block, though people sometimes use wood offcuts for the sanding block. It should be moved along the wooden object in *straight* lines, working with the grain. Alternatively, you could use a portable sander. You should also treat any knots before considering the final finish.

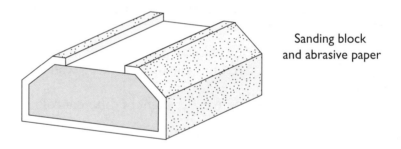

Sanding block
and abrasive paper

Timber can be finished with one of the following:

- **Paint**
  Before painting roughen the surface so that the paint has something to grip. It also helps to degrease the surface with white spirit. Start with a primer, which you should allow to dry before applying an undercoat. It is a good idea to brush the top coat in the opposite direction to the undercoat. Between paintings you could rub down the wood with a fine glass paper as this should improve the finish.
- **Polish**
  French polish is a traditional finish. It can be applied with a brush or a cloth. It should be put on in thin layers and can be rubbed down between coats, leaving many hours for drying.
  If wax polish is used then it should be applied more heavily and left for several hours. It can be put over French polish and gives more protection, as well as a shine.
- **Varnish**
  Polyurethane is widely used on furniture as it is tough, heatproof and waterproof. It is applied like paint and rubbed down between coats, again leaving several hours for drying.

- **Oil**
  Teak or linseed oil can be used to give a more natural finish. You should rub in small amounts with a soft dry cloth to enhance the grain.
- **Stains**
  Hardwood finishes are popular because they are attractive and have low maintenance costs. In contrast, creosote is practical but unattractive and strongly smelling. However, it does soak deep into the wood.

FINISHING PLASTIC

There is less need for finishing with plastic because its robustness means that it needs less protection. However, there are three ways of finishing once a plastic surface has been filled:

- **Abrasives** can be used – a 'wet and dry' type is advisable.
- A **buffing machine** (and soap) can smooth and shape plastic. However, this should only be done with permission and under supervision by a teacher.
- **Metal polish** can be applied to achieve a polished surface.

FINISHING METAL

The finishing required varies with the nature of the metal.

Ferrous metals, such as steel, need to be protected from *rust*. Steel may be well finished on a lathe or a milling machine. Any machining marks can be removed with *emery cloth*, starting with rough grades and advancing to fine finishers.

Paint can be used with metal, as with wood. The main difference is that metal surfaces need degreasing with paraffin and then washing with detergent. Also different primers might be used.

A **buffing machine** could also be used, as could **metal polish.**

Non ferrous metals, such as copper, will not rust but can *tarnish*. This can be prevented by using a coat of protective *lacquer*. It can be applied with a brush.

A high standard of finish can be achieved by using a 'wet and dry' abrasive or pumice powder (very fine abrasive) worked in with a damp cloth.

FINISHING TEXTILES

The finish largely depends on the function of the item. For example, a three-piece suite can be stainproofed by using Scotchguard to preserve its quality and prevent food stains damaging its appearance. Curtains can be sprayed to make them fire retardant or backed with an aluminium-based reflector to facilitate heat retention.

With many textiles the nature of the seams and facings can enhance the finished product.

10 SYSTEMS AND CONTROL

The Great Gatsbow's Financial Emporium:
The Original Mechanical Cash Dispenser

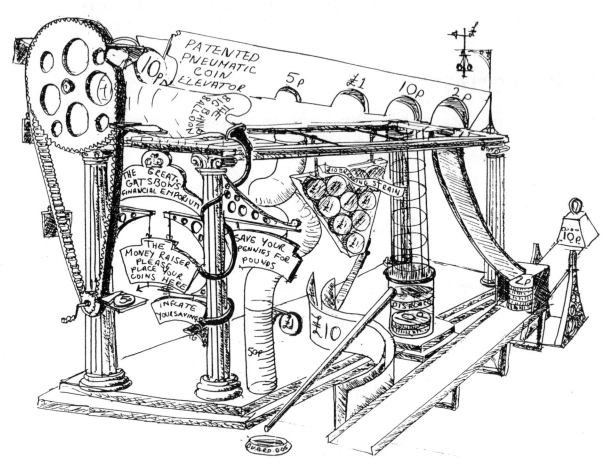

This Victorian-style cartoon provides a light-hearted view of this topic. If you study the drawing carefully then you should be able to understand the principles of systems, sub-systems and control. However, before we ponder the amusing logic there is a need to understand what we mean by the terms used so far.

A **system** is a set of devices or things which are connected and work in conjunction with each other in order to perform a specific function.

Examples:

Our railway system allows trains to travel from one city to another without the driver having to think where he is going. The train is processed by signal operators who control the points at which the train can change tracks.

Musical instruments such as trumpets and bagpipes are pneumatic systems which allow pressurized air to escape through various sized holes.

A printed circuit board (PCB) – the type you see in modern radios and television sets – is an electrical system which connects different components together.

A **sub-system** is simply a small system inside a large one.

We use the term **control** for the means by which outcomes can be predetermined.

It is also important to understand that there are several forms of system. We can have, for example:

– mechanical systems
– electrical systems
– pneumatic systems

All systems have an INPUT PROCESS and an OUTPUT.

This is the way we think about systems. Consider the cartoon for a moment. Here we see a coin poised in the 'patented pneumatic coin elevator'. Before the coin can be processed, however, the elevator needs to be raised. This is achieved by pumping air into the system via the mouthpiece (see the sign about inflating your savings). From this we can conclude that:

       AIR   is the INPUT (this is fed via the tube up to the balloon)
INFLATION   is the PROCESS (of the balloon)
ELEVATION   is the OUTPUT (of the coin elevator)

This then is a way of looking at the pneumatic system. There is of course also a mechanical output to this system. That is, when the angle of the coin sorter is steep enough to cause the coin to roll over the coin stop (which is a control device in its own right) we have an output of 'motion' from the coin.

Now test yourself

Complete the sentences below.

The input is when the **(a)** .... – .... is used to raise the coins up to the top of the emporium. The process part of this system is when the coin tray starts to **(b)** .... and **(c)** .... a vertical position. If you look back at the coin tray at the bottom, where we started, you should notice the coin is fitted onto a wedge. This wedge will of course become a ramp when vertical and so provide a means by which the coins can roll. The output is therefore one of **(d)** ....

The answers are on p. 78

Now we should consider the coin elevator and sorter. This we call a control system and by looking closely at the construction of it you should be able to detect how the coins are controlled.

If you are not able to understand the logic by which the device works then take a few coins from your piggy bank and compare them. You should be able to see that while the coins have some things in common, they also have some characteristics that are different.

Now test yourself

One factor that these coins have in common is that they are all **(e)** ....

Other characteristics which are different are (choose one for each letter):

(f) .... smell, thickness, rigidity

(g) .... diameter, shape, texture

(h) .... conductivity, density, volume

(i) .... weight, decoration, value.

The answers are on p. 78

Of course there are also differences such as colour but these characteristics are not developed or exploited in The Great Gatsbow's Financial Emporium. This is really the key to understanding control systems – that is, being able to identify characteristics which can be used to distinguish or sort out the coins.

Below is an orthographic drawing of the sorter. You could have some fun if you made one from an old piece of card. All you have to do is cut a piece of card (from a breakfast cereal box or shoe box), then fold the card along its length. Position the coins so that they are exactly halfway over the fold and then draw round them with a sharp pencil and cut the holes out. Now you are in a position to try rolling coins down the sorter from either direction. You could also try to vary the angle of the V.

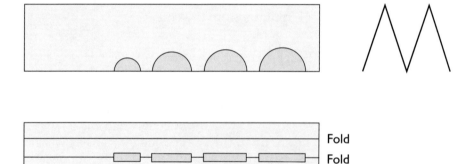

Fold
Fold
Fold

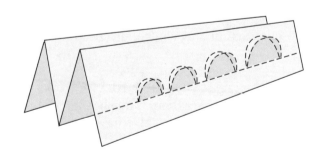

As you can see, when the coins roll down the slot they encounter a series of different sized holes. Then, because each type of coin is a different size (5p the smallest, 2p the largest) the coins will either pass over the hole or, if they are smaller than the hole, drop through and enter another system.

So what prevents the 5p or £1 coin dropping through the 10p hole and entering the 10p sub-system? The answer is the order in which the holes are arranged. Would the coin sorter work if the holes were positioned in a different sequence?

Earlier we established some similarities and differences in the coins. *The fact that all the coins are the same shape is important for it enables them to be processed by the same mechanism.* As an obvious contrast in shape, consider how a square coin might perform, then consider a 50p piece.

Of course a square coin could not be processed by this method since it would not roll. There is also another reason why it could not work. This is because the coin would not have a diameter. Cut a square of card of appropriate size and see how many holes it will pass through. 50p and 20p coins are almost circles so that might give a clue as to whether or not they could be processed.

Having analysed the function of the coin sorter we are now able to turn our attention to the four sub-systems. Each of these sub-systems works by exploiting the characteristics of that coin, identified in the questions above. Can you find out which one is which? Below is a description of each system.

Under the 5p slot is a tube which carries the coins off to the bottom where they sit neatly on top of one another. Marked on the side of the tube are gradations which indicate when 50p or £1 has been saved.

Below the £1 slot is a triangular 'see through' hopper. This collects the coins and stacks them on edge. You should notice that the hopper is suspended by string and chain. The string is like fishing line and has a specific breaking strain. When this breaking strain is reached the hopper tilts and allows the coins to roll down the £10 slot.

Below the 10p slot is a cage which ensures that the coins drop into the displacement can at the bottom. This displacement can is filled with water up to the level of the tube.

Below the 2p slot is a chute which carries the coins off to a weighted balance. Coupled to the balance is another chute which directs the savings towards the cashier's point.

From these descriptions and from looking at the cartoon you should now be able to conclude that the 5p controlled banking and counting system works because each coin is the same thickness.

The system that involves the £10 hopper is a bit of a trick. From the label you are made to think about pounds in weight and then link this to pounds in money value. It would be more accurate to state that the breaking strain of the string would be ten times the weight of a £1 coin. This should then be given in kg and g. The shape of the hopper also needs to be considered for this is a control device. This stacks the coins in the order seen because the hopper has been designed according to the diameter of the coins. Thus when the hopper is full and the string snaps, all the coins roll out.

The 10p system works on volume. Each time a coin drops through the hole into the displacement tank, it sinks to the bottom and pushes its own volume of water up to where it can run down the tube. This gives the guard dog a drink.

Finally the 2p system works on weight so that when the total weight of the coins ($5 \times 2p$) is saved the balance tilts and the money is sent down the chute.

Through this cartoon you have been given an introduction to systems and control. Try to think of other devices that could be incorporated into the emporium.

11 STRUCTURES

Structures are built to support loads. They can vary from something simple such as a drawer to complex structures such as suspension bridges.

The loads on any structure are either *static* or *dynamic*. Static loads do not move, e.g. books on a bookshelf, whereas dynamic loads produce much greater forces, e.g. cars on a bridge.

Structures can be *frames* or *shells*. A *shell* takes the load on the *inside*, whereas a *frame* takes it on the *outside*. For example, a garden chair is a shell which supports a load, but a bed is a frame structure.

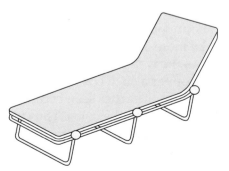

There are many *forces* which act as structures. You need to understand these when you are designing a structure.

Compression – this is the squashing of a structure, e.g. someone standing on a ladder.

Tension – this is the stretching of a structure, e.g. steel wires on a suspension bridge.

Bending – here compression and tension work together. When a gymnastic bar is being used, there is compression on the upper surface and tension on the lower part. An excessive weight may cause a structure to bend and then buckle.

Torsion – this type of force twists a structure.

Shearing – this cuts a structure in two, e.g. a pair of scissors.

Designing structures

When designing a structure, it is often a good idea to start with a model. The different parts of a structure are called *members* and they often cope with different forces. *Beams* are a common kind of structural member: the illustration shows an 'I' beam but there are also 'L' and 'T' shapes. Generally the widest section of the beam should take the load. The shape will also determine the structural properties. For example, if a beam is hollowed out it becomes more rigid and lighter.

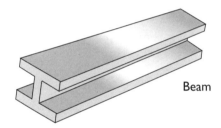

Beam

Rectangular shapes are vulnerable to heavy loads so a good idea is to add an extra member to give stability. Such an addition strengthens the structure by creating two *triangles*, as shown in the illustration below.

A weak point in most structures are the *joists*. These can be strengthened by bracing them with short members, called *gusset plates*.

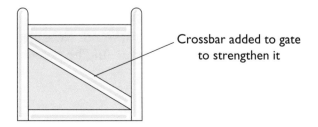

Crossbar added to gate
to strengthen it

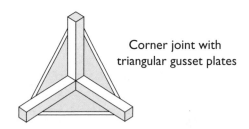

Corner joint with
triangular gusset plates

These additions all help to reinforce the structure. If you look at different types of household furniture you can see examples of such strengthening techniques.

12 QUALITY

The best quality does not necessarily mean the most expensive, as is often the case in business. It means that something 'cannot be bettered' in the circumstances, with the equipment available at our level of production.

There are several criteria which enable us to judge the quality of a product:

- whether it meets a clear need
- its fitness for the purpose
- whether the appropriate resources are used
- the external effects of its use (i.e. if it has an impact over and above its intended use) on the environment

If we take a simple pencil as an example of a product, we can see that it meets a need for a writing instrument. It is easy to handle, light and effective. When it starts to go blunt it can be sharpened. The fact that it gradually diminishes in size until it is too small to use does not really matter because pencils are very cheap. Appropriate resources such as wood and carbon are used in the manufacture of pencils which are mass produced. There are no adverse affects from using pencils: they do not generate pollution, for example.

Clearly a pencil is a good example of a *quality design.* In addition, the six-sided shape means that information about the product and the maker's name can appear on it. Being easy to paint it can have a colourful finish and thus be attractive to potential buyers. It can be made aesthetically pleasing.

However some pencils are not of good *quality manufacture.* We have all come across 'cheap' pencils where the paint flakes off, the writing point breaks easily and sharpening is difficult because of the wood. Note also that if toxic paint were applied as a finish then the product would be potentially very harmful.

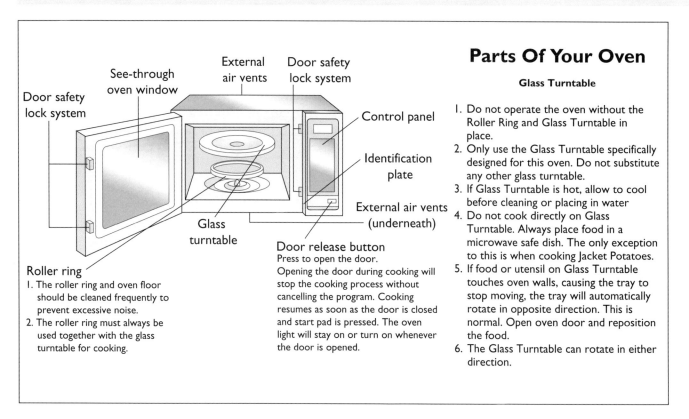

Parts Of Your Oven

See-through oven window

External air vents

Door safety lock system

Door safety lock system

Control panel

Identification plate

External air vents (underneath)

Door release button
Press to open the door.
Opening the door during cooking will stop the cooking process without cancelling the program. Cooking resumes as soon as the door is closed and start pad is pressed. The oven light will stay on or turn on whenever the door is opened.

Glass turntable

Roller ring
1. The roller ring and oven floor should be cleaned frequently to prevent excessive noise.
2. The roller ring must always be used together with the glass turntable for cooking.

Glass Turntable

1. Do not operate the oven without the Roller Ring and Glass Turntable in place.
2. Only use the Glass Turntable specifically designed for this oven. Do not substitute any other glass turntable.
3. If Glass Turntable is hot, allow to cool before cleaning or placing in water
4. Do not cook directly on Glass Turntable. Always place food in a microwave safe dish. The only exception to this is when cooking Jacket Potatoes.
5. If food or utensil on Glass Turntable touches oven walls, causing the tray to stop moving, the tray will automatically rotate in opposite direction. This is normal. Open oven door and reposition the food.
6. The Glass Turntable can rotate in either direction.

As a contrast to the pencil, let us consider the microwave oven. This product is a recent invention which meets the need of people today to spend less time preparing meals. Most meals made in microwave ovens take a fraction of the time spent cooking in the traditional way. The food which is produced is fit for human consumption, assuming the operating instructions are carefully followed.

The microwave oven requires a large capital outlay. Most are made of steel with zinc coating which is very durable. They are electrically operated with extensive control panels which provide a variety of functions, such as defrosting and calorie counting. Furthermore, they are compact and not heavy (the example shown here measures 530 mm × 366 mm × 356 mm and weighs 16 kg).

However, there are a few minor impacts. For example, an operating microwave can cause interference with a TV set (this is also true of some other household electrical appliances). Warm air is emitted from the oven vents, though this is relatively insignificant as there are no microwaves in this air. A final concern might be what happens to a microwave once it has reached the end of its working life. For example, it might be dumped and so become an eyesore.

Standards of quality

We made the distinction earlier between the quality of design and the quality of manufacture. There is a system for the latter called *British Standards*. The microwave oven illustrated was produced to BS 800. As well as conforming to these external specifications, firms have their own internal processes to check the standards of workmanship. This is known as *quality control*. Since products cannot always be perfect, manufacturers allow *'tolerance'*. For example, there will be very small tolerance limits for the parts of a microwave because they have to fit together and move.

13 HEALTH AND SAFETY

This has become an increasingly important issue for designers, makers and consumers. Manufacturers are liable for any adverse effect of their product on a person. Retailers have an obligation to consumers to replace, repair or refund money if products are not 'as described', 'of merchantable quality' or 'fit for the purpose' (Sale of Goods Act). Any of these deficiencies would indicate a lack of quality in manufacture.

Safety in the home

Consumers need to take care with the increasingly sophisticated products that are being developed. A good starting point is to read the operating instructions provided by the maker of a product. Not only should the instructions be read but they should be kept for reference. They usually contain key safety information. See the operating instructions for a microwave below.

Important Information – Read Carefully

Short Cooking Times

As microwave cooking times are much shorter than other cooking methods it is essential that recommended cooking times are not exceeded without first checking the food. Cooking times given in the cookbook are approximate. Factors that may affect cooking times are: preferred degree of cooking, starting temperature, altitude, volume, size and shape of foods and utensils used. As you become familiar with the oven, you will be able to adjust these factors. It is better to undercook rather than overcook foods. If food is undercooked, it can always be returned to the oven for further cooking. If food is overcooked, nothing can be done. Always start with minimum cooking times.

Important.

If the recommended cooking times are exceeded the food will be spoiled and in extreme circumstances could catch fire and possibly damage the interior of the oven.

1. Small quantities of food.

   Take care when heating small quantities of food as these can easily burn, dry out or catch on fire if cooked too long. Always set short cooking times and check the food frequently.

   NB. If materials inside the oven should ignite, keep oven door closed, turn oven off, and disconnect the power cord, or shut off power at the fuse or circuit breaker panel. **NEVER OPERATE THE OVEN WITHOUT FOOD INSIDE IT.**

2. Foods low in moisture.

   Take care when heating foods low in moisture, e.g. bread items, chocolate, biscuits and pastries. These can easily burn, dry out or catch on fire if cooked too long.

3. Christmas Pudding.

   Christmas puddings and other foods high in fats or sugar, e.g. jam, mince pies, must not be overheated. These foods must never be left unattended as with overcooking these foods can ignite.

4. Boiled Eggs.

   Do not boil eggs in their shell in your microwave. Raw eggs boiled in their shells can explode causing injury.

5. Foods with Skins.

   Potatoes, apples, egg yolk, whole vegetables and sausages are examples of food with non porous skins. These must be pierced using a fork before cooking to prevent bursting.

6. Liquids.

   When heating liquids, e.g. soup, sauces and beverages in your microwave oven, overheating the liquid beyond boiling point can occur without evidence of bubbling. This could result in a sudden boil over of the hot liquid. To prevent this possibility the following steps should be taken:

   a) Avoid using straight-sided containers with narrow necks.
   b) Do not overheat.
   c) Stir the liquid before placing the container in the oven and again halfway through the heating time.
   d) After heating, allow to stand in the oven for a short time, stirring again before carefully removing the container.

Safety in the workshop

As there are a lot of variable factors here, there are many safety elements to be considered if accidents are to be avoided.

Human behaviour

Don't 'mess about' when making things.
Concentrate on what you are doing.
Know where the first aid kit is kept (just in case!).
Be careful about how you carry equipment around, for example don't carry sharp instruments with the point dangerously exposed.
Keep the work place tidy.
Never work alone in the workshop.

Clothing

Wear protective clothing (and eye protection when required).
Don't wear loose clothes or fashion shoes.
Remove jackets, ties and jewellery.
Tie back long hair, roll up sleeves.

Housekeeping

Tidy up regularly, not just at the end of a lesson.
Clean machines after use (if necessary) and put away tools.
Keep any exit/gangway clear in case a hasty exit is needed.

Tools

Keep tools in good condition (i.e. sharp if appropriate).
Use tools in the correct way and for their intended purpose.
Replace tools in racks provided.
Report any damages to tools to your teacher.

Materials

As metal, wood, textiles and plastics have different properties, the precautions that need to be taken vary. Plastics should be kept away from naked flames. Most chemicals should be used in well-ventilated areas. Waste material should be disposed of as your teacher instructs.

Machines

Learn and understand how a machine operates before you begin to use it.
Get permission before you start.
Before starting a machine, check that all the safety precautions have been taken, e.g. guard lowered, eye protection put on.
If you wish to adjust your machine, switch off first and send for your teacher.

Answers to Now test yourself

Page 50

1   With rope and a strong stick.

2 Put two drawing pins into a suitable surface about 10-15 cm apart. Then put a loop of string around them. Pull tight with a pencil and rotate around the pins.

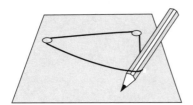

Page 51

4 Possible answers: clothes peg, sugar tongs, hair grip, food tongs.

5 Possible answers: carving dish, magnetic soap dish.

Page 53

6 Holding meat together, testing to see if the middle of a cake is properly cooked.

Pages 69 and 70

(a) turning-handle (b) tilt (c) assumes (d) motion (e) round (f) thickness (g) diameter (h) volume (i) weight

---

L EVEL DESCRIPTIONS: MAKING

At the start of Key Stage 3 the majority of pupils will have reached at least Level 4 in Technology. By the end of Key Stage 3 most pupils should be within the range of Levels 4–7. Levels 5–6 are the target for 14-year-olds. Level 8 is the standard reached by very able pupils.

Use our checklist to assess the Level reached, by ticking the skills that have been mastered.

Level 4

☐ When designing and making, produce step-by-step plans that identify the main stages in making, and list the tools, materials and processes needed.

☐ Measure, mark out and cut simple forms in a variety of materials and join them using a range of techniques.

☐ Show increasing accuracy, paying attention to quality of finish and function.

☐ Identify what is, and what is not, working well in the products.

Level 5

- [ ] When designing and making, work from the plans produced, modifying them in the light of difficulties.

- [ ] Use a range of tools, materials and processes safely with increasing precision and control.

- [ ] Use measuring and checking procedures as the work develops, and modify the approach if first attempts fail. Evaluate the products by comparing them with the design intentions and suggest ways of improving them.

Level 6

- [ ] When designing and making, produce plans that outline the implications of design decisions, and suggest alternative methods of proceeding if first attempts should fail.

- [ ] Become increasingly skilful in the use of the techniques and processes identified in the Key Stage 3 Programme of Study, and use tools and equipment to work materials precisely.

- [ ] Evaluate the products in use and identify ways of improving them.

Level 7

- [ ] When designing and making, produce plans that predict the time needed to carry out the main stages in making, and match the choice of materials and components with tools, equipment and processes.

- [ ] Adapt methods of manufacture to changing circumstances, providing a sound rationale for any deviations from the design proposal. Select appropriate techniques to evaluate how the products would perform in use and modify them to improve their performance.

Level 8

- [ ] When designing and making, produce plans that identify where decisions have to be made.

- [ ] The plans should allow for alternative methods of manufacture.

- [ ] Organize the work to ensure that processes can be carried out accurately and consistently, and use tools and techniques with the degree of precision required by the plans.

- [ ] When evaluating the products, identify a range of criteria that address issues beyond the purpose for which the product was designed.

Exceptional performance

- [ ] When designing and making, produce and work from plans that specify how each stage in the making is to be achieved and that make best use of the time and resources available.

- [ ] Work to a high degree of precision to make products that are reliable and robust and that fully reflect the quality requirements and detail given in the design proposal.

- [ ] Devise evaluation procedures, use these to indicate ways of improving the products, and implement these improvements.

CHAPTER 3
*I*nformation technology

I NTRODUCTION

In Key Stage 3 technology, information technology (IT) is vital. This chapter will therefore answer some basic questions about IT. Several of the assignments which feature the information technology aspect of Key Stage 3 require a knowledge of IT skills. Doing these exercises will help you to gain confidence with IT.

At the end of this chapter there are sections which explain how to set up a data base and a spreadsheet. These sections go into detail with tips and examples to show how they can be developed.

Throughout this chapter the applications of IT are considered. Examples are given from both school work and the business world.

W HAT IS IT?

Information technology is quite simply the keeping, changing and obtaining of information by electronic means. Information can be in the form of words (text), numbers (data), music (sounds) and pictures (images).

A computerized photograph is a digitized image. It can be 'manipulated' in lots of different ways such as changes in size, shape, proportion and colour. Because the picture exists as points of light on a television monitor every aspect of the picture can be changed. This is done by switching some of the points of light off and others on. You can do the same with text and data.

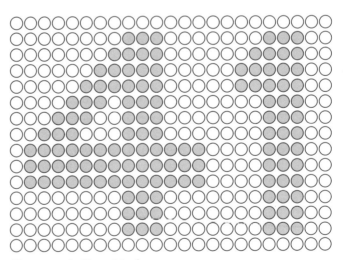

Close up of a 'Starvision' screen.
These types of screens work in the same way as computer montors

Most people think that IT is just about computers and nothing else. Computers are of course a large part of IT but so too is video equipment, cassette tape recorders and photocopiers. All of these can perform the tasks of creating, keeping and changing information.

WHAT USE IS IT?

In the world of work it is now quite difficult to find a large-scale production process that does not involve a computer. Not only do these machines save vast amounts of time and money but they also create lots of new possibilities by linking people and information together. If you think again about the ability to manipulate information then in terms of design this means that all sorts of possibilities can be tried very quickly and easily. Once an idea has been drawn and stored in a computer then it can be changed many times. Traditionally a designer had to create a separate drawing for every idea developed.

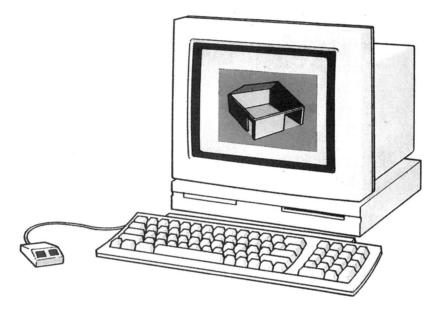

H OW CAN YOU LEARN ABOUT IT?

This is best considered as two aspects:

① As a need to learn with IT.
② As a need to learn about IT.

Learning with IT

Information technology can improve learning situations. Originally, educational opportunities were devised so that pupils could respond to various questions set by a particular computer program. Depending on the answer given, a pupil could be rewarded with another set of questions. This kind of program tended to be linked with one particular subject area. However, as the 'hardware' (the computer) developed so too did the 'software' (computer programs). The trend these days is to present pupils with software packages which are not linked or limited to one particular subject. Instead you can use the technology to develop and improve your own work.

Word processing is a good example of how IT provides you with opportunities to correct spelling mistakes and to change the composition of your work and then to print out your 'copy' to a professional standard. This kind of software can be used in any subject where you have to produce written work.

Other very useful software is the 'art' or 'graphics' type. Simple graphics, such as bar charts and pie charts, can be generated from a software package rather than being drawn freehand. There are also art programs which enable you to paint computer pictures, and change and reposition images.

This kind of software is very useful for experimenting with different variations of the same design, for example, for a company logo. However, the same software can also be useful for developing electronic circuit diagrams or different kinds of geographic maps. In both of these cases symbols are drawn and then stored.

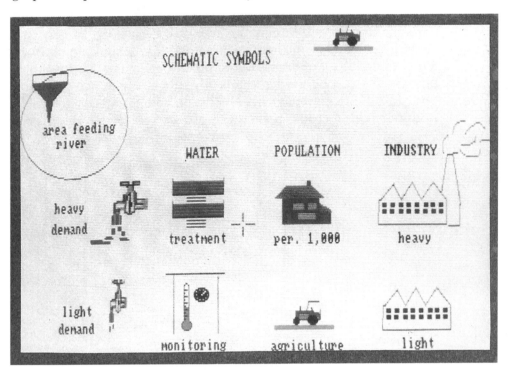

The same symbols are then assembled into diagrams and maps. In each case the symbol is only drawn once but can be used any number of times.

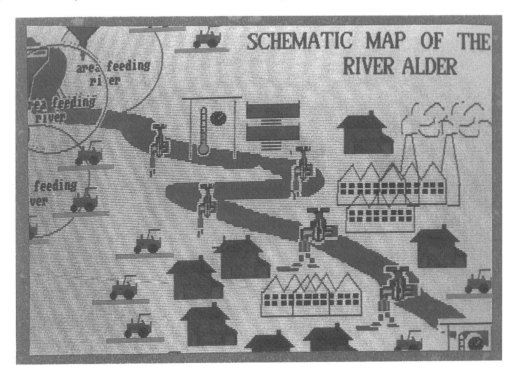

This type of application not only saves time but also puts an end to having to do the boring job of drawing the same thing over and over again. Desktop publishing packages offer a similar function. This kind of software often has a library of 'clip art' (standard pictures) which you can select and use with blocks of text. By the time you reach the end of your third year at secondary school, you will have been taught how to use this software.

Information technology can be used in many subjects, such as geography, history and maths. In fact IT helps to link the subjects together. In doing this IT improves the quality of education. This is because IT provides you with many more choices whilst at the same time providing specialist knowledge and skills. The result of all this is that your work, like essays, projects and artefacts, can be completed and presented to a very high standard.

Learning about IT

A few years ago learning about IT would have entailed learning all sorts of obscure computer commands in order to make the machine do what is now considered to be a fairly easy task. Happily this is no longer the case. As the technology has become more and more powerful then so some of that power has been used to make the machines easier to use (more 'user friendly').

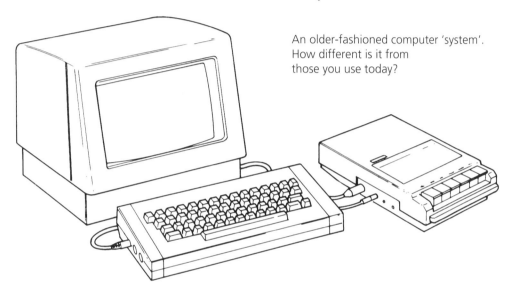

An older-fashioned computer 'system'.
How different is it from
those you use today?

Complicated, meaningless commands are no longer required. Instead the operator simply positions a pointer on top of a picture and presses a button. This is what we do today; tomorrow it will be made even easier!

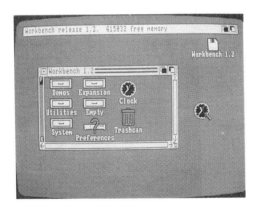
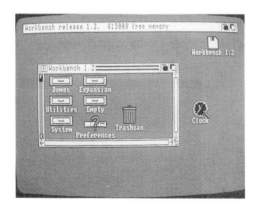

Commands are issued simply by positioning the pointer over the appropriate picture and clicking a button on the mouse

There is no point in learning detailed procedures, these are specific to each type of machine and will become out of date very quickly. It would be far better to understand general principles and to become aware of what the technology can do. That way you can develop an understanding which will enable you to decide when a computer is the best tool for the job. These skills are transferable, from one machine to another, and from one task to another. This is learning about IT.

WHAT KINDS OF SOFTWARE DO YOU NEED TO KNOW ABOUT?

There are several types of software packages of which you should have an understanding. It is not necessary for you to understand them in every detail. All you have to know is the kind of functions that the software can perform and how to operate them at a simple level.

The most important types of software are:

1. Word processing.
2. Graphics.
3. Desktop publishing.
4. Control.
5. Data bases.
6. Spreadsheets.

You will probably have come across some of these software applications before. It will be useful to understand a little of what they can do.

1 WORD PROCESSING

Word processing is quite easy to understand. On a simple level it is just typing text into a machine. Taken further it is the means whereby you can change and 'play with' the text. This can be done in many ways.

Letters, words, sentences and even whole paragraphs can be inserted or removed. It is also possible to split up lines and to change the appearance of the text. Similarly the width of the text can be altered. Words no longer have to be split up and hyphenated from one line to another because the computer can constantly readjust the spacings between the words on a line so that the type appears in neat columns. Once a document has been produced it can be stored and then altered for another use.

Let's suppose that you want to apply for a Saturday job at one of eight local supermarkets. If, instead of writing the same letter eight times, you word processed your application, the main body of your letter would only have to be produced once. It would then take only the simple matter of altering the name and address at the top! There are, of course, 'mail merging' programs that do this automatically.

The young technologist at work

Think of other situations where using a word processor would save you the time and bother of having to write something out several times.

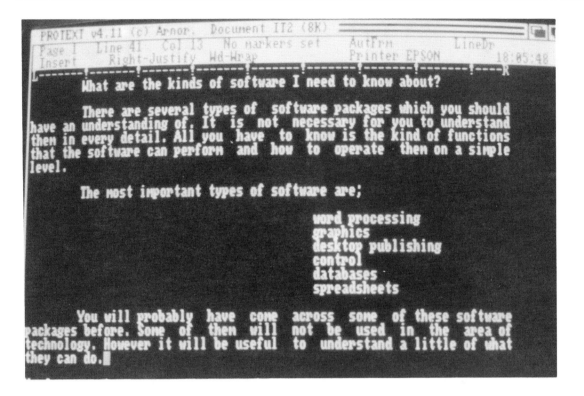

Some of the more complex word processing software can offer some quite clever functions. These include the ability to hunt down words or phrases in a document and change them for others. Similarly very long words or phrases which are used often, rather like the word 'technology' in this book, can be made to appear with a press of just one key – there's no need to keep typing the word out! Other functions include checking for spelling mistakes, offering alternative words, and giving dictionary definitions and advice on correct grammar and punctuation. One software package will even grade your work and tell you how easy your work is to read and understand!

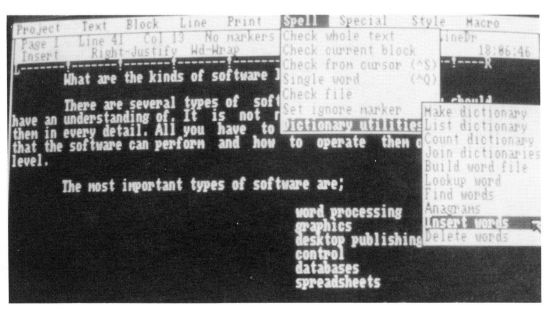

2 GRAPHICS

There are several types of graphic software which you can use depending on the type of image you wish to produce and the way you wish to process it.

The Delux 'Point III' in use

Probably the most widely used types of graphics package are the 'arts' ones. All of these offer similar functions which allow you to draw in several ways. Controlled by either a mouse or a joystick, images can be constructed from a variety of types of line and shapes. Colours can be 'sprayed on' or 'filled' with quite remarkable effects. However, perhaps the most impressive aspect of this kind of software is the ability to copy part of a picture, however small and complicated, and turn it into a kind of 'magic paint' with which you can perform all the functions already mentioned.

As with other computer functions one of the most successful applications is the copying of effects. Repetitive patterns are therefore easily and rapidly reproduced. Size, shape, colour and position can be changed instantly and then immediately changed back again. Textile and wallpaper patterns have never been easier to design because designers now have the technology to try lots of ideas that may be only slightly different.

Painting with points of light is an established fine art technique. Here it is done on a computer

Like word processing, the more complex packages can perform additional functions, such as animation. With these packages it is possible to wrap flat images on to an imaginary package which can then be made to appear to move!

Computers are well suited to graphic 'commercial' art

All sorts of pattern generation is now possible at the push of a button

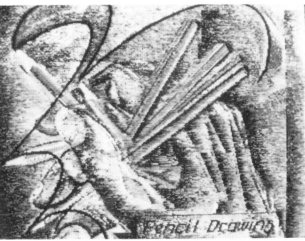

The same basic picture developed in two different ways. This is where computers are very useful

The final type of graphics software that should be mentioned is what some people call CAD (Computer Aided Design) packages. These are used in the production of technical drawings. Here again traditional equipment such as rulers, compasses, dividers, set squares and slide rules have all been replaced by the use of software. Very accurate diagrams and drawings can be produced relatively quickly. If mistakes are made, however serious, they can be rectified very easily, while dimensions can be included automatically. The same drawing can appear with imperial measurements (feet and inches) or with the metric equivalent by just pressing a key. As with all the other software, there are opportunities for change and alteration.

More complex versions of this kind of software can, from simple elevations (a side view, an end view and a plan), produce three-dimensional images which can then be made to rotate. Designers, therefore, can view the object from any angle. Images can be coloured, shaded, and even have textures added and made to look very realistic. Other functions include the ability to 'model'. This means that objects can be built up from a series of contours, rather like the way mountains appear on a map. This is sometimes called 'wire framing'. When complete the object can then be made to appear solid as though made from one of a number of different materials such as wood, metal, plastic and glass.

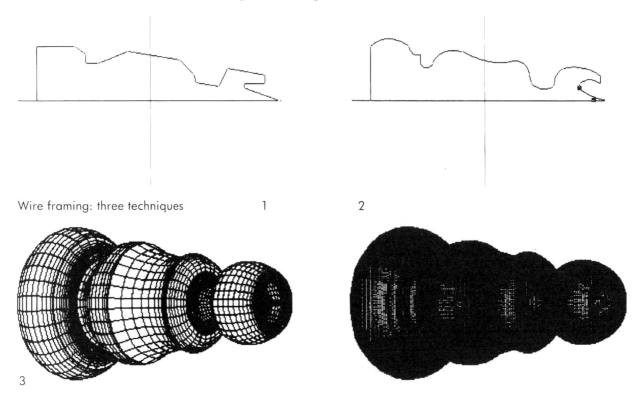

Wire framing: three techniques   1   2

3

Conversion of wire-framing into solid modelling

These examples were produced on a simple home computer using free software

3 DESK TOP PUBLISHING

This is another type of software, known as DTP, and is a combination of the word processing and graphic types of packages previously described. This type of software, therefore, provides the opportunity to combine text with pictures, and is the kind of software which is used to produce newspapers. It is very clever in the way that it makes blocks of text appear in a variety of different lettering styles. The shape and size of the blocks of text can be varied. These articles together with the illustrations can then be positioned in any desired combination on the page. A common phrase used to describe this function is 'cut and paste' which is an accurate description of what really appears to be happening! Even more complex varieties of this kind of software allow photographic images to be processed. Software of this type is very popular with the students who use it in the production of projects and coursework. The standard of presentation can be very high if there is access to a good printer.

4 CONTROL

You will, perhaps, have come across this type of software in other subjects (maths, for example) because it has much to do with numbers and figures. With this kind of software it is possible to issue electronic instructions to other devices in order that certain functions can be performed. These functions can be calculations or measurements such as temperature or strain. Alternatively the software can be used to control robots, like those used in the motor industry. It is known as CAM (Computer Aided Manufacture) and can be highly complex to operate. However, it can be seen in very many junior schools in its simplest form where it is used to control a robotic toy turtle! You may see it in your secondary school because you may have computer controlled machinery such as a lathe, a milling machine or a sewing machine which does embroidery. It is also possible that the school heating is monitored and controlled by a computer. Micro-processors, which are really only small computers, are used in the control of many domestic appliances such as electric kettles, TV sets and washing machines.

 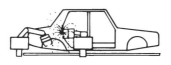 

I T WINDOW

SCREEN SHOTS
(computerized colour images without a printer)

Although you may have a computer you may not have a printer. Alternatively you may have a black and white printer but would like colour images. Here's how to get round the problem by taking photographs of the images that appear on the computer screen. You can also use this process for taking photographs of images from the television but the picture must be absolutely static.

To produce the best results you should use a camera where you can adjust the speed of the shutter. This should be set to 1/8th of a second or less and the aperture set accordingly. If you understand camera techniques you should get a reasonable result with a shutter speed of one second and an aperture of F11.

If you are using an automatic 'compact camera' good results should still be possible. You must, however, mount the camera so that it is absolutely rigid, preferably on a tripod. The centre of the camera lens must be in line with the centre of the screen and as close as the focusing of the camera will allow. The screen needs to contain a good range of colours – large amounts of black and white should be avoided. Finally the room needs to be completely dark with the screen being the only source of light.

Some of the photographs included in this book have been achieved in this way!

5 DATA BASES

A data base is a **collection of information** about a subject. For example, your school library will have a catalogue of its books, usually saved in a card index system. Each **card** in the **index** will have a reference number, the title of the book and its author. It may also contain other information such as the date of publication and the name of the publishers. In modern public libraries all this information is kept on a special data base called a 'microfiche'. Here the information is stored on very small 'slides' allowing an enormous amount of information to be kept on a simple transparent sheet and then displayed on a screen.

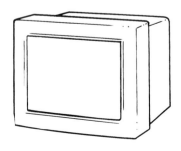

Records and fields

A data base is like a filing cabinet containing many **files.** Each file is called a **record** and each record is subdivided into **fields.** Thus, in the library books example above, each book is a record. The different types of information stored about each book are its fields. So, one field is the book's title, another is its author, and so on.

The number of records and fields in a data base will depend on two things: firstly the capacity of your computer package and secondly the detail which you wish to store.

Fields should always be given a **title**. There are *different types* of fields possible in most data base packages. A computer needs to know the type of information to be stored in each field. Most packages include the following types of field:

❶ **Numeric** – these contain digits and are used for **calculations**. Decimal points can be specified too. They are useful for pounds and pence, for example.
❷ **Alpha** – these contain alphabetic characters and can be used for names. They can also include numbers 0-9 for use with addresses and telephone numbers but they cannot be used for calculations.
❸ **Date** – these contain space for six or eight digits so that the date can be included. It is usually set DD/MM/YY: day, month and year.

Setting up a data base

There are *three* stages in setting up data bases:

❶ Defining a file structure.
❷ Entering the data.
❸ Manipulating the data.

The following explanation applies to the Mini Office Professional Package for an Amstrad. The techniques may be slightly different with other software but the process is largely the same.

1 *Defining a file structure*

You must first decide what **information** you wish to store in your data base. This will determine what records you keep and how you organize them. The organization of the information is called the 'file structure'. This means:

– stating the **field names**, e.g. name
– specifying the **contents** of the fields, e.g. person's surname followed by other names
– deciding how much **space** to give each field, e.g. number of characters: 30
– selecting the correct **type of data** for each field, e.g. alpha

The structure and, in particular, the space for each field need planning in advance. This means thinking about the information and its possibilities. The following shows four fields for a personnel file:

```
name       :   Martin A
sex        :   f
birth date :   03/03/1960
salary     :                17800

name       :   Tolhurst V
sex        :   f
birth date :   21/8/1939
salary     :            28200
```

```
name          : Teacher M
sex           : f
birth date    : 28/10/1935
salary        :                    60000
```

```
name          : Klute G
sex           : f
birth date    : 05/05/1942
salary        :                    10600
```

2 *Entering the data*

A data base usually begins by displaying empty fields into which you should enter the data. The **cursor** is placed at the first character position on the first field to indicate where the data should be entered.

The **four arrow keys** ($\uparrow \downarrow \rightarrow \leftarrow$) are used to move the cursor from field to field and between characters within one field.

Many changes can be made to data once it is entered. For instance, if you enter the wrong number, it can be **deleted**. Similarly, **new** information can be added to the fields, and existing records can be changed **(edited)**. You can move between records, usually by using a **'GOTO'** instruction.

Once you have the necessary information correctly entered, you should **save** all the records by selecting the 'save' option. The information can be **displayed** in whole or in part, as you wish. It can obviously be **printed** as necessary, as shown below.

```
name          : Smith P
sex           : m
birth date    : 04/05/1948
salary        :                    19500
```

```
name          : West K
sex           : m
birth date    : 11/06/1946
salary        :                    19500
```

```
name          : Martin A
sex           : f
birth date    : 03/03/1960
salary        :                    17800
```

```
name          : Link C
sex           : m
birth date    : 12/12/1940
salary        :                    82000
```

```
name          : Tolhurst V
sex           : f
birth date    : 21/08/1939
salary        :                    28200
```

```
name        :  Lynch M
sex         :  m
birth date  :  16/02/1957
salary      :                  16500
```

```
name        :  Teacher M
sex         :  f
birth date  :  28/10/1935
salary      :                  60000
```

```
name        :  Klute G
sex         :  f
birth date  :  05/05/1942
salary      :                  10600
```

3 Manipulating the data

This process involves looking at the entered data in different ways. Most software packages enable you to do three things with a data base:

(a) Search the information.
(b) Sort the information.
(c) Make calculations.

(a) Searching

You may want certain specific information from your data base. For example, information on all female employees earning over £13 500 (average UK male earnings) from a payroll file. You will need to instruct the data base to select and mark such records. The search will produce the necessary information and it can then be printed out.

(b) Sorting

You may want to organize the presentation of your information in a certain way. For example, you may not have entered the data alphabetically but want it in this form. So you can select the 'sort' function from the menu to do this.

(c) Calculations

You can make a simple calculation which can be applied to all the records. For example, you could show the effect on the payroll, if everyone was given a 10 per cent salary increase. You would need to alter the marked records.

The following shows a search and sort of our small data base. The data has been put into alphabetical order and just the female employees have been selected.

```
name        :  Klute G
sex         :  f
birth date  :  05/05/1942
salary      :                  10600
```

```
name        :  Martin A
sex         :  f
birth date  :  03/03/1960
salary      :                  17800
```

```
name       :  Teacher M
sex        :  f
birth date :  28/10/1935
salary     :                    60000

name       :  Tolhurst V
sex        :  f
birth date :  21/8/1939
salary     :                    28200
```

6 SPREADSHEETS

These are not as frightening as they sometimes appear. They are simply a way of making quick calculations on figures put into a computer. The information can be displayed in several different ways too, depending on the software package used. The **table** format is most commonly shown, as below, but **graphics** can be used to display data in a pictorial way.

	A	B	C	D	E	F	G	H	I
001			NUMBERS	ATTENDING					
002			10	20	30	50	100	200	500
003	PRICE		5	5	5	5	5	5	5
004	TOTAL	REVENUE	50	100	150	250	500	1000	2500
005									
006	COSTS								
007									
008		fixed	50	50	50	50	50	50	50
009		variable	60	120	180	300	600	1200	3000
010	TOTAL	COSTS	110	170	230	350	650	1250	3050
011									
012	PROFIT or LOSS								

Setting up a spreadsheet

There are three stages involved in creating a spreadsheet:

1. Planning the layout.
2. Entering data, text and formula.
3. Producing the output.

1 *Planning the layout*

The layout of your spreadsheet should first be planned on file paper or **graph** paper. It is really a model to avoid later mistakes. When planning how to lay out your spreadsheet it is a good idea to use a **pencil** and have an **eraser** handy. This is because you are likely to change your pattern as you think more about it!

You have a two dimensional matrix, as below, on which to plan your spreadsheet. Ignore the highlighted section for the time being.

```
        A . . . . . . B . . . . . .

001
002
003
```

(a) *Rows and columns*

Your data needs to be organized in **rows** and **columns**. A spreadsheet usually identifies columns with letters and rows with numbers. The size of the spreadsheet depends on the data which it is going to hold. It is really just a **grid** of information. For example, if you wanted to show the various sales of a local shop on different days, you could let the columns represent days and the rows represent the goods sold.

If more than 26 columns are needed you could start column 27 with an 'AA' reference.

```
     A ...... B ...... C ...... D ...... E ...... F ......
001           Mon      Tues     Wed      Thurs    Fri
002
003  Mars
004  Twix
005  Yorkie
006  Crisps
007  Coke
008  Cartons
```

(b) *Cells*

A **cell** is the space where a row intersects with a column. This is shown on the previous page. It is referred to by the combination of a column letter and row number. The cell highlighted here is 3B. The highlighted cell is known as the **active** cell because it can be filled with data, text or formulae.

The cursor keys ($\uparrow \downarrow \rightarrow \leftarrow$) are used to move from one cell to another. The cell references are sometimes called the **co-ordinates**, being just like the squares on a graph you might use in a maths lesson. However, these cells are often rectangular in shape.

2 *Entering data, text and formula*

The data entered on your spreadsheet will be **numbers**. The text or **words** will describe parts of the spreadsheet. The formula or **instructions** will enable quick calculations to be made on the data.

(a) *Data*

Putting the data on the spreadsheet is often a tedious exercise but it needs to be done! You must be *consistent* in what you do. For example, if some data are whole numbers and others are decimals, then all must be shown in decimal form. Thus 17 becomes 17.00.

Sometimes if you want to put the same number for each cell in the row, you can save time by using the copy facility. The operation of copying varies between the software programs used but it is always quite a simple operation.

(b) *Text*

The words used on the spreadsheet are usually for **headings**. At the start it is a good idea to give the rows and columns headings. The size of each cell on the grid needs to be considered carefully. For example, if the cell extends to seven letters and your heading exceeds that length, you will need to extend the cell on the grid or abbreviate the heading.

(c) *Formula*

A formula on a spreadsheet is just a simple piece of maths. It is a way of telling a spreadsheet what to do with the data which you have entered. Using simple maths formulae enables the quick *calculation* of certain results.

For example, as shown below, you can instruct the computer to add fixed costs to variable costs to obtain a figure for total costs. As the total required is in cell C10 you instruct it, by giving it a formula, how to calculate the total cost. So in this case the formula would be C8 + C9.

A	B	C	D	E	F	G	H	I
001	NUMBERS ATTENDING							
002		10	20	30	50	100	200	500
003 PRICE		5	5	5	5	5	5	5
004 TOTAL	REVENUE	50	100	150	250	500	1000	2500
005								
006 COSTS								
007								
008	fixed	50	50	50	50	50	50	50
009	variable	60	120	180	300	600	1200	3000
010 TOTAL	COSTS	110	170	230	350	650	1250	3050
011								
012 PROFIT or LOSS								

On most packages you can insert the formula fairly easily and get it repeated for other cells quite quickly. If the entering is done properly, the word 'functi' is shown in the cells to indicate that a formula has been given. It is usually a good idea to note the formula used on a piece of paper with the relevant cell references. In the above example it would be C10 = C8 + C9.

3 *Producing the output*

Once you have put the data in the cells and the formulae in other cells, the spreadsheet will make calculations based on logic and simple mathematics. Then you programme the spreadsheet to update and convert the formula (functi) to actual calculated numbers, and results. Shown above is the final calculation made in our simple example.

Finally, the display below shows how easily new information can be inserted. If fixed costs change for every level of output to 70 then, once this data is entered, the spreadsheet can be instructed to recalculate the totals using the original formula.

A	B	C	D	E	F	G	H	I
001	NUMBERS ATTENDING							
002		10	20	30	50	100	200	500
003 PRICE		5	5	5	5	5	5	5
004 TOTAL	REVENUE	50	100	150	250	500	1000	2500
005								
006 COSTS								
007								
008	fixed	70	70	70	70	70	70	70
009	variable	60	120	180	300	600	1200	3000
010 TOTAL COSTS								
011								
012 PROFIT or LOSS								

L EVEL DESCRIPTIONS: IT CAPABILITY

At the start of Key Stage 3 the majority of pupils will have reached at least Level 4 in Information Technology. By the end of Key Stage 3 most pupils should be within the range of Levels 4–7. Levels 5–6 are the target for 14-year-olds. Level 8 is the standard reached by very able pupils.

Use our checklist to assess the Level reached, by ticking the skills that have been mastered.

Level 4

☐ Use IT to combine different forms of information, and show an awareness of audience.

☐ Add to, amend and interrogate information that has been stored.

☐ Understand the need for care in framing questions when collecting, accessing and interrogating information.

☐ Interpret findings, question plausibility and recognize that poor quality information yields unreliable results.

☐ Use IT systems to control events in a predetermined manner, to sense physical data and to display it.

☐ Use IT-based models and simulations to explore patterns and relationships, and make simple predictions about the consequences of decision making.

☐ Compare the use of IT with other methods.

Level 5

☐ Use IT to organize, refine and present information in different forms and styles for specific purposes and audiences.

☐ Select the information needed for different purposes, check its accuracy and organize and prepare it in a form suitable for processing using IT.

☐ Create sets of instructions to control events, and become sensitive to the need for precision in framing and sequencing instructions.

☐ Explore the effects of changing the variables in a computer model.

☐ Communicate knowledge and experience of using IT and assess its use in one's own working practices.

Level 6

☐ Develop and refine work, using information from a range of sources, and demonstrating a clear sense of audience and purpose in presentation.

☐ Where necessary, use complex lines of enquiry to test hypotheses.

☐ Develop, trial and refine sets of instructions to control events, demonstrating an awareness of the notions of efficiency and economy in framing these instructions.

☐ Understand how IT devices can be used to monitor and measure external events, using sensors.

☐ Use computer models of increasing complexity, vary the rules within them, and assess the validity of these models by comparing their behaviour with other data.

☐ Discuss the wider impact of IT on society.

Level 7

☐ Combine a variety of forms of electronic and other information for presentation to an unfamiliar and critical audience.

☐ Identify the advantages and limitations of different data-handling applications, and select and use suitable information systems, translating enquiries expressed in ordinary language into forms required by the system.

☐ Use IT equipment and software to measure and record physical variables.

☐ Design computer models or procedures, with variables, which meet identified needs.

☐ Consider the limitations of IT tools and information sources, and of the results they produce.

Level 8

☐ Select the appropriate IT facilities for specific tasks, taking into account ease of use and suitability for purpose.

☐ Design and implement systems for others to use.

☐ Design successful means of capturing and, if necessary, preparing information for computer processing.

☐ When assembling devices that respond to data from sensors, describe how feedback might improve the performance of the system.

☐ Discuss in an informed way, the social, economic, ethical and moral issues raised by IT.

Exceptional performance

☐ Evaluate software packages and complex computer models, analysing the situation for which they were developed and assessing their efficiency, ease of implementation and appropriateness.

☐ Suggest refinements, and design, implement and document systems for others to use, predicting some of the consequences that could arise.

☐ When discussing own and others' use of information technology, relate understanding of the technical features of information systems to an appreciation of how those systems affect wider social, economic, ethical and moral issues.

CHAPTER 4

Problems and assignments

There are sixteen short problems and five longer assignments. They are in the order in which you should tackle them.

SHORT PROBLEMS

The problems get harder as you work through the chapter. The first few tasks should refresh your memory and may act as revision of the work you will already have encountered in class. The later ones should make you think a bit more and are quite demanding. Each task has its National Curriculum Level shown, so that you can see how difficult it is meant to be. It also says 'Design', 'Making' or 'Information Technology' to show you which kind of task it is.

These assignments require **you** to **do** things: so do them! The task you are to do is indicated by a ⬚ symbol. If clues are offered in order to help start you thinking these are indicated by a ⬚ symbol. You will find that some of the assignments are followed by a sample answer. This answer highlights the important skills which in technology are expected of you and which should be shown in your answer (these are printed in blue).

Design – Level 3

B EDROOM PLAN

You need to be able to investigate a familiar context, such as your home, for design and technological opportunities. In this exercise assume that it is your bedroom. Below is a detailed plan with the door and window shown. Specific measurements have been given and scale models of a bed, a table and a wardrobe are shown.

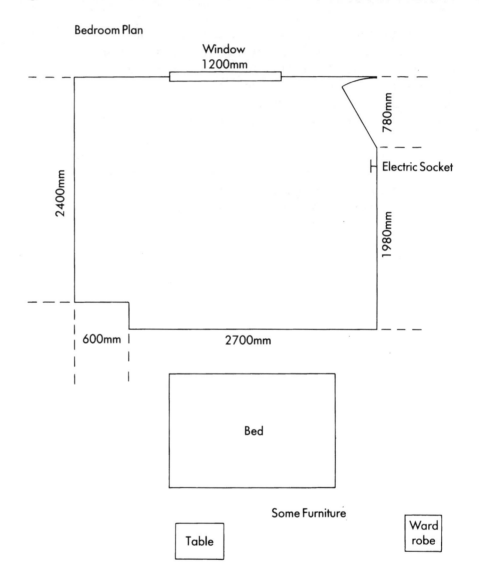

Design your ideal bedroom, using the plan and the scale models in order to help you.

You could start by asking yourself 'What do I use my bedroom for?' For example, is it also used as a study? Also consider in detail things like the type of wardrobe to be used, the means of storage, the electric socket and other bedroom furniture. All this will make a difference to your design.

It might help you either to cut out the models reproduced above, or to make copies of them, so that you can move them around the bedroom plan. Any extra furniture should be drawn to the same scale, so that you can test if all the required things can fit into the room together.

A sample answer

I have decided to organize my bedroom as shown below. In addition to the bed, table and wardrobe it has a clothes basket and bookcase. As I use my bedroom for quiet studying sometimes, a bookcase would be helpful. I could possibly also have a desk or worktop which could, maybe, double as a dressing table. It is, in fact, very similar to my actual bedroom at present. However, I realized that it was a good idea to position a built-in wardrobe along one of the walls in order to save space. I chose to use the shortest wall.

I decided to put my bed near the wall opposite the window. This enables me to have plenty of space in the centre of the room. I did not cover the electric socket as it will need to be accessible for hairdryers, vacuum cleaners and so on.

In planning my ideal bedroom, I asked my elder sister and my father for their views. In addition, I looked at home magazines and some catalogues.

Develop idea about possible needs

Suggest practical changes with reasons

Use results of investigations

Describe familiar surroundings

Use knowledge from a familiar situation

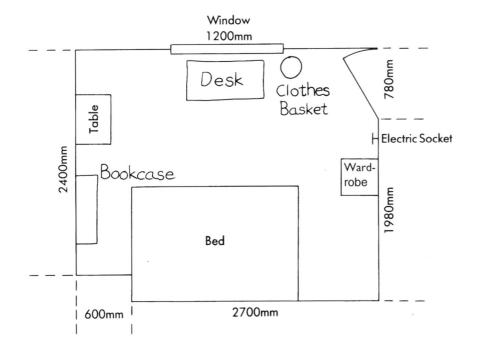

101

Design – Level 4

B IRD SCARER 1

The drawing (below) of the scarecrow shows the traditional way of frightening birds away. The second drawing is a 'low tech' solution to the same problem but because it uses only discarded milk bottle tops it is on a smaller scale. It might be used in a back garden or on an allotment. It is different because it is aural rather than visual. The blowing wind generates a noise which in theory discourages birds from settling and eating crops. The rotating gun in the third drawing is more 'high tech'. It is especially manufactured for the purpose and combines constant movement with a frequent loud bang!

 Design a 'bird scarer' which is fairly cheap yet effective. You will need to use models and/or drawings to illustrate your design proposal.

Here are some things you could bear in mind:

– colours
– source of power
– type of material
– size
– weight
– shape

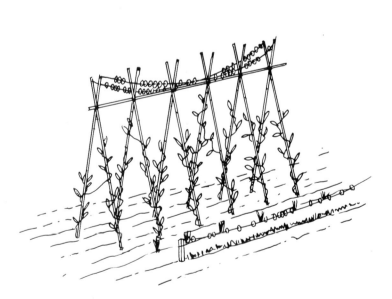

A sample answer

Reasons for design

Apply knowledge to select idea

Use of information about people

My answer to this problem is a 'big bird kite'. Many of the birds which attack crops are medium-sized like **starlings, sparrows** and **blackbirds.** Thus, they might be frightened off by a bird of prey such as a **sparrowhawk** (see below). A kite that closely resembles such a bird of prey and is mobile would thus probably be effective. The kite, once set up, could be fixed to one spot and perhaps moved regularly so that other birds did not realize that it was inanimate. The most colourful bird of prey could be chosen so that it stands out and can be easily seen.

Design proposal

Use of information

The kite would need to be made out of a hard-wearing material, which does not rip easily and resists the rain, e.g. plastic laminate. The lines to which it is fixed would need similar qualities. It would need to be quickly assembled and dismantled because farmers would not wish to waste valuable working time. Also, its smallness would allow easy storage.

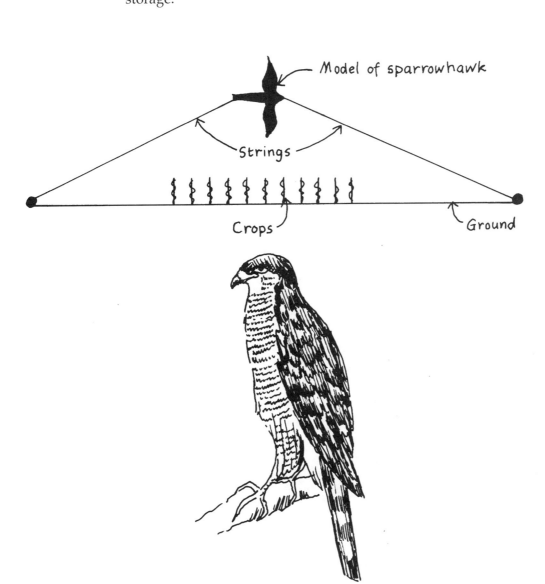

Design – Level 6

S UNHAT 1

In July and August 1990, Britain had some of its hottest days for over fifty years. The extract from the *Guardian* newspaper below gives some evidence of this heatwave.

Britain in July

West lets the sun shine in

Michael Hulme reviews
last month's weather

DAYTIME TEMPERATURES: The average national daytime temperature was higher than usual every day for the last three weeks of July, with the 19th being the hottest day with 23.8°C. Temperature anomalies were negative only along parts of the east coast of England. Western Britain generally had the largest positive anomalies — more than 2°C.

RAINFALL was below average. Only the far north of Scotland and the Isle of Man received more than average, while southern and eastern England received less than 40 per cent of normal. But the first week of July was very wet, averaging more than 30mm.

SUNSHINE: After a cloudy June, sunshine was abundant. Many places received more than twice their June averages and, as a whole, Britain received 40 per cent more. Plymouth and Guernsey received more than 10 hours a day while Folkestone and Ross-on-Wye enjoyed a few minutes less.

Dr Michael Hulme is a Research Climatologist at the University of East Anglia.

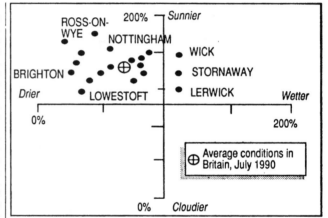

July 1990: Warm, and very sunny

Daytime temperature	1.3°C above average
Rainfall	69 per cent of average
Sunshine	140 per cent of average

(all average figures are based on the 1951-80 average)

Absolute extremes:

Warmest	Ross-on-Wye	24.0°C
Sunniest	Plymouth	318 hours
Wettest	Eskdalemuir	96 mm
Coldest	Lerwick	14.1°C
Cloudiest	Lerwick	137 hours
Driest	Skegness	12 mm

However, many people do not like the hot sun on their head and neck, even though they enjoy getting arms and legs suntanned!

Your task is to design yourself a *cheap suitable sunhat*. There are some existing examples below, for inspiration! You should consider:

– sketches of the sunhat
– materials needed
– breaking the task into parts
– planning the order of work
– drawing diagrams to scale

A sample answer

Record of ideas showing how they are classified and developed

Ideas – colourful, simple, rim and top, soft, velcro, two-piece, easy to fold, carry, elliptical shape.

Sketch

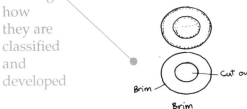

Brim

Brim — Cut out

Brim

Top

Combine various aspects of the design

The two basic parts will need to be of different materials. The rim should be stiffer so that it does not flop down over the wearer's eyes. The top should be soft and flexible so that it can fit around different shaped heads. The two fabrics could be in different colours so that the hat is attractive.

Explain why idea not used

On further examination of different hats, it was decided that making just two parts was not possible. Although the brim could be one piece,

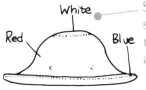

Side 1

Top

Side 2

Top needs to be in several parts so that it curves down to the brim

Design proposal

the top would need to be in several parts as shown, with Side 1 and Side 2 joining the top to the brim. However, this could give scope for three or four different coloured pieces.

Seek out and organize information to develop ideas

Having looked at books about sewing, magazines, patterns, and existing hats, my final sunhat is as follows:

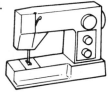

White

Red

Blue

Specify what should be done by using simple plans and diagrams

There are four holes (eyelets) to allow for ventilation. The four pieces are drawn to scale pattern and slightly overlap to allow for machining. The material used should be light, probably cotton. By making the brim of double thickness cotton, machined together, it is stiffer than the top. (My original idea of two different fabrics was not feasible.) The sides need to be trapezium shaped. This allows the circumference of the top to be smaller than the inside of the brim, so giving a more natural head shape. The brim should be hemmed, both on the outside and inside edge. Machine stitching to be used throughout at the joins, and also every quarter-inch around the surface of the brim (see the plans on the next page).

Refine design proposal

Check availability of resources and adapt design as necessary

A running stitch can be used for plain seams. The cotton should be the same colour as the piece upon which it shows. Thus blue cotton should be used on the blue brim.

Availability of resources

I realize that I shall need the following **equipment** to do all this: scissors or pinking shears for cutting the material, pins for holding pieces in place, and a sewing machine.

P ROPAGATOR 1

Greenhouses and garden frames are **systems** which protect seedlings and cuttings. They are also **environments** which speed up the growth of crops and plants. In doing this they are acting as 'propagators'.

You do not have either of these *artefacts*. Your garden is not big enough for a greenhouse and no one is interested in looking after one anyway. A garden frame would be too vulnerable as the garden is mainly used for playing ball games.

You have been given some lettuce seeds and so need a *propagator* which is small enough to put on a large window ledge inside the house. You need to develop a design proposal and produce a design specification.

Consider the following:

– number of plants to go into the propagator
– height to which plants will grow
– suitable materials
– will the propagator need heating?
– what types of propagators can you buy?

A sample answer

The propagator shown **(1)** could be used with or without electric heating. It could use a soil-warming cable and control unit, which includes a thermostat to control the temperature.

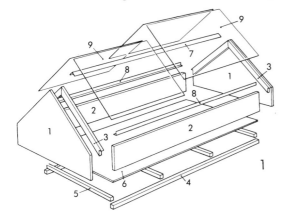

Alternatives suggested

(1) is a photocopy of a design which I found in *The Readers' Digest Complete Do-It-Yourself Manual*. I have modified it in several ways. For example, I shall use cling film instead of glass. In addition, the model above was too large and so mine has been designed much smaller, needing fewer component parts. My final design is shown in **(2)**.

Use information from different sources

Combine ideas

Question 1

Review details of the design

2

The parts specification is given on page 121 (it forms the basis of that exercise).

The hardware needed would be 20 mm no. 6 counter-sunk screws.

Parts list						
Number	Name	Quantity	Long (cm)	Wide (cm)	Thick (cm)	Material
1	End panel	2	30.5	See p.121	0.92	Hardboard
2	Sides	2	76.25	15.25	1.52	Hardboard
3	Bottom	1	76.25	29.3	0.6	Hardwood
4	Top piece	1	76.25	0.6	0.6	Dowel rod
5	Cross battens	3	25.5	1.85	1.85	Hardboard

These dimensions are finished sizes.

Question 2

Construction should occur in the following order:

Ways of reaching chosen outcome

Cut the end, bottom and side panels to length (see page 121). Join the bottom to the side panels as shown on page 121. Then glue and screw the cross battens. Next fix the end panels flush to the ends of the bottom and sides. Finally, screw the dowel rod to each of the end panels. The cling film can be applied tightly over the wooden structure.

Question 3

Question 4

This design should fit the requirements of the user and it is cheap and quick to make.

1 What are the advantages of using cling film rather than glass?
2 Why should you order material slightly larger than that actually required?
3 How can the cling film be fixed so that it can be lifted up and put down again, without tearing?
4 Is this sample answer complete?

Design – Level 7

C HOOSING GLUE

In this exercise, assume that you are a teacher with a budget to spend on supplies. You have recently received the advertising material shown below.

You have to decide whether or not to buy Rollits or the usual glue. Write a brief report outlining your decision with reasons.

Here is further information on the Rollits:

'The Rollit adhesive applicator lays a 12 mm strip of glue just where you need it, simply press and pull. The adhesive is in three grades:

(a) Permanent for instant sticking.
(b) Lift-off, which stays stuck to the first surface you apply it to and reveals a "post-it note" type of adhesive for **temporary** sticking.
(c) Rub-off, which may be removed from both sides after use by simply rubbing with a finger.
The refills are easy to fit.'

Consider the following questions. They should help you to write your report.

What existing products are there?
Can Rollits be tested?
Compare the advantages and disadvantages of Rollits.
Is the cost reasonable?

A sample answer

Review needs
identified and
decide if
appropriate

The report
This includes answers to the four questions given as clues on the previous page.

The Rollit seems to meet a definite need, as students often stick things together. If the advertising copy is correct, then the product seems appropriate. There are many existing competing products, such as Gloy or Pritt. The Rollit is similar to Pritt in that it does not need a brush or spatula to apply it.

Devise and
carry out tests

I cannot test it to see if it works. It should work, because if not, the firm can be prosecuted under the Sale of Goods and/or Trade Descriptions Acts. I could buy one this year and see how it works, before committing myself to a bulk order.

Evaluate ways
in which
materials have
been used

Evaluate
procedures
and
processes

It is certainly different from other adhesives. It is **versatile** and flexible and could be used instead of 'stick-it' labels. The visual **appearance** is attractive and its name nicely describes how it works. Also, it has a bit of a toy **image** as well as appearing cleaner than existing sticking agents. The **finish** looks smooth. However, the **durability** has to be taken on trust, as does the ease of inserting refill tapes.

The first illustration gives some idea of how it works. However, **reliability, accuracy** and **speed of use** can only be judged by using it. Nevertheless, it seems less messy than the old-style glue bottle and **storage** is probably easier. There is no danger of glue sniffing! It may be more technologically advanced than Pritt.

Economic
consequences
of innovation

The biggest problem though is the **cost**. It would need to be substantially better than existing adhesives for it to be value for money. This is because it is more expensive, even without the applicator, as shown below:

Product	Price (£)
Rollit	0.89
Pritt	0.60
Gloy gum	0.35 (5.3 fluid oz)
Glue pen	0.49 (50 ml)

I cannot comment on the reaction of students and/or suggest improvements to the product until I have bought it.

Gather
information
about
product and
reactions of
users

Design and Making – Level 7

MOTORWAY SIGNS

Study the following two pieces of correspondence sent to the technical director of McWimpys and then the technical director's response to his research department. It all concerns **motorway temporary signs**.

RAC
1 July 1995

Dear Sir,
Temporary Road Signs

Our patrol officers are very unhappy about temporary road signs used on your motorway roadworks. They are not clear at night time and not very stable, particularly in windy conditions. Several officers have noticed that many of these signs get blown over when it is blustery. At present many small sacks filled with sand are used to weight down the signs.

These deficiencies have made roads dangerous at times to approaching motorists, as they are not aware of the hazards that may be facing them.

Yours faithfully,

A. Driver

MEMORANDUM

From: Site Manager, M180
To: Technical Director   1 July 1995

Temporary Road Signs
We are having the following problems with these:
1 They are difficult to store.
2 They easily fall over.
3 They are not very effective in high winds. Bags of sand are used to weight them down but it is wasting time having to keep putting these bags out and collecting them in again.
4 Theft of signs is increasing – are they collectors' items now?

MEMORANDUM

From: Technical Director
To: Research Department

Temporary Road Signs
Please read the enclosed two pieces of correspondence.
Can you come up with a better design?

Can you come up with a better design for the temporary road signs than the existing one?

The existing temporary road signs are shown below.

Are the existing signs heavy enough?
Are the existing signs a suitable shape?
Are the existing signs stable enough?
Are the existing signs clear?
Could existing signs be modified or is a new design specification needed?
What materials are required and why?
How should a new sign be constructed?
Is ease of storage important?
What budget is available?
What sort of tests would be needed for a prototype?

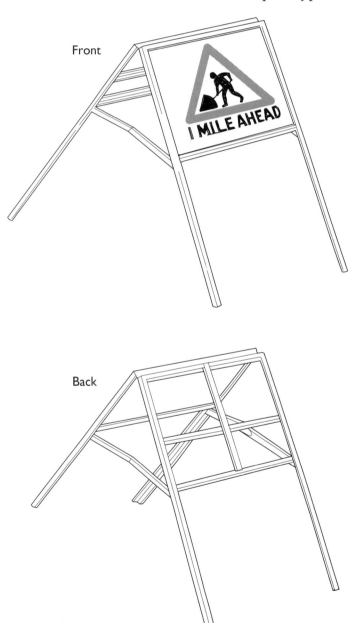

Front

I MILE AHEAD

Back

Can you make a small-scale model of your design?

Design – Level 7

LY KILLER

In this exercise you need to pretend that you are a home owner, who has to make a spending decision. You are faced with a plague of flies in your house. This is as a result of a long warm summer, local farming practices and pollution from a nearby food factory.

You have to choose which of the three following fly-killing remedies to buy. Consider the advantages and disadvantages of each as the best solution to your fly problem.

1 A can of fly spray (not containing CFCs) – cost £1.00

Directions: shake well before use and spray room for up to five seconds.
Precautions: do not breathe in spray, wash hands after use, do not spray onto food, keep in safe place. Extremely dangerous to fish.
Warning: pressurized container. Protect from sunlight, store in temperatures less than 50°C. Do not pierce or burn after use.

2 Flypapers – four for £1.20

Directions: warm tube if cold. Pull out slowly with twirling motion. Hang away from sunshine and draughts.

Flypapers are non-toxic and therefore absolutely safe to use.

Our slogan: 'Give your flies a sticky end!'

3 Fly swat – 50p

There are no directions, precautions or warnings with this 'weapon'! Its success depends on human hand and eye co-ordination.

How long will each fly killer last?
Which is the safest?
How are they stored?
Is any of them an 'eyesore'?
How are the dead flies disposed of?
Which remedy costs most in the long run?
Are they all equally effective in each room?

Which gives best value for money?
How long does each take to operate?
How long does each take to work?
How much effort is involved on your part?
Will the use of the fly killer affect other people?
Does the fly killer get in the way?
Is it fashionable?

Some further tasks

1 If you could not go shopping, what alternative solutions could you think of?
2 How would you test which of the three products is most effective?

Making – Level 4

B IRD SCARER 2

This is a practical solution to the bird scarer problem on p.102.

Colour in the bird shapes shown, cut them out, then mount them onto something strong. Finally, fix them together.

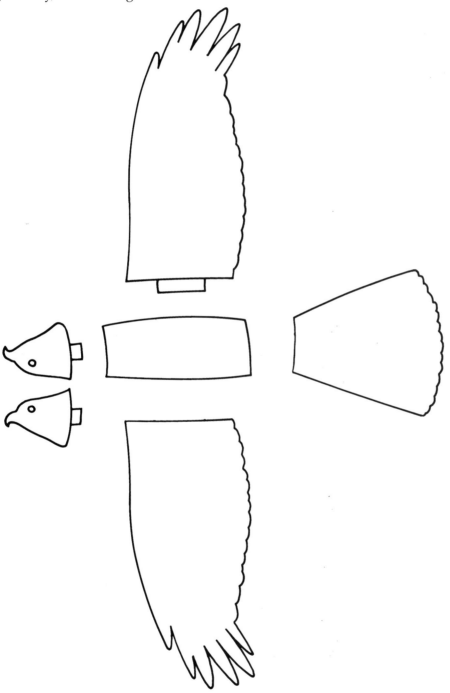

 Choose the appropriate equipment, materials and fixing agents needed to create a two-dimensional model of a sparrowhawk. Consider the problem particularly of assembling the shapes, very carefully before you start. For a three-dimensional model you would need a suitable stuffing for filling out the shape into its correct form. Consider what could be used for this purpose.

The finished article should be a properly constructed model resembling a sparrowhawk!

A sample answer

These are the skills you should have demonstrated:

Use of simple
hand tools

- – cutting out the pieces accurately using scissors
- – colouring the parts of the bird using crayons, felt-tipped pens or paints
- – mounting the paper onto card or another suitable material, using glue, sellotape or staples

You will probably have **planned** the sequence of events for construction of the bird scarer. For example, if your plan included colouring before cutting out give yourself a pat on the back because when drawing and colouring it is usually easier to operate with larger pieces of paper rather than smaller ones.

Consider available
resources

When mounting the paper onto a firmer surface you may have been limited in your **choice of materials** – cardboard is fairly easy to get hold of, e.g. cereal packets, whereas plastic is less so, e.g. drinks containers.

Choose appropriate
resources

Regarding your fixing of the paper you should have been guided into choosing the correct fixative by the characteristics of the two surfaces to be stuck together and the many different types of glue. When using paper, liquid glue is unwise because it seeps through. 'Pritt', on the other hand, is more suitable. You may have considered using sellotape or staples but each is inadvisable in this case because both produce an untidy finish.

A deliberate difficulty was included in this problem. Did you spot it? Tabs have been put on only some of the cut-out pieces! This should have created an unforeseen difficulty to which you needed to respond. You could have got around it in several ways including redrawing the pieces *with* tabs, or using staples to fix the untabbed pieces together (although, as already stated, staples do have some disadvantages). Alternatively, you might have devised another way. What was it?

Improvise

Making – Level 5

C REME EGGS

It is Easter. You have some Cadbury's Creme Eggs and want to give them as Easter presents to your friends. You want to give them in boxes. However, you bought all your Creme Eggs loose!

Make a suitable box for containing two Creme Eggs.

On the next page you are given the plans for the making up of the box. It is in two parts because one page would not be big enough to take the shape whole. However, when using this shape to trace onto your chosen material make sure the material is big enough to take both 'parts' of the shape shown – that is, so that you can make up the box in **one piece**. Points A and B need careful lining up when you trace the shape onto your material. **Do not cut along A-B** – it should be a fold!

What material will you use?
Where can you get it from?
What is the maximum size of the shape to cut out?
What equipment is needed?
Can you work out which fold needs sticking?
What can be used to fix the flaps?
Which parts will be inside the box?
Where will the opening be?
Is colour needed on the outside?
Is anything required inside the box to protect the eggs?
Do you need to use a surface finish?
Which way up will you store the eggs?

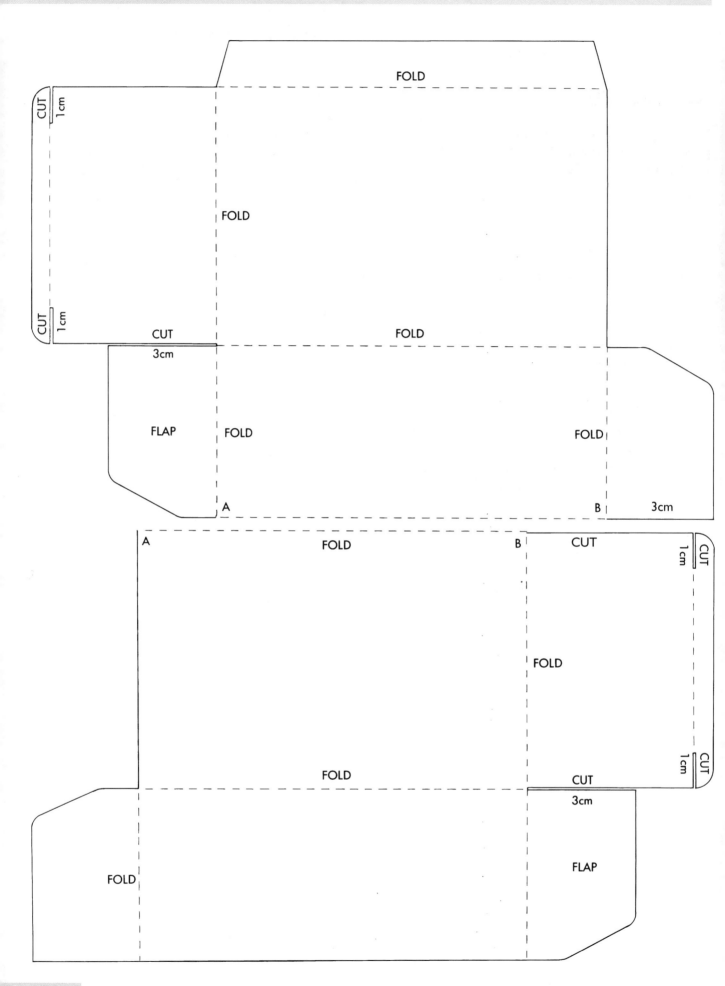

Making – Level 6

C AT BASKET

Your family has decided to have a pet cat. In order to save money, you have made a basket for it to sleep in, out of a cardboard box.

In addition, there is the further matter of deciding where to put the 'basket'. Four possibilities have been suggested:

– in the garage
– in the kitchen
– in the lounge
– in your bedroom

 You have to decide which is the best place for the basket. On the next page an approach is suggested.

 Will it be a dangerous place for the cat?
Will the cat be a nuisance to me or others in the family?
Is the cat near its food?
Will the cat disturb people at night?
Will the cat bring mice in?
How much space is needed?
Will the cat be warm enough?
Will the other furniture in the house suffer?
Will the cat's 'basket' look out of place?
Will the cat's 'basket' be an eyesore?
What do other people do with their cats' baskets?
Will the cat damage things?
Will the cat's basket get in the way?
Will the cat be tempted by human food?
What do the rest of your family want as the solution?

Use the table below to consider the advantages and disadvantages of each place.

Bedroom	
Advantages	Disadvantages

Lounge	
Advantages	Disadvantages

Kitchen	
Advantages	Disadvantages

Garage	
Advantages	Disadvantages

Before making your final decision, you perhaps need to weigh up which are the most important of the factors. For example, one place may have more advantages than the others but those advantages may be fairly unimportant. On the other hand, it may only have one disadvantage but this could be of major significance. By considering such things you should end up making a **quality** judgment, rather than one based on just **quantity.**

In my house the best place would be ....

Making – Level 7

S UNHAT 2

Below are the scale drawings for a type of sunhat suggested in the assignment on p.104.

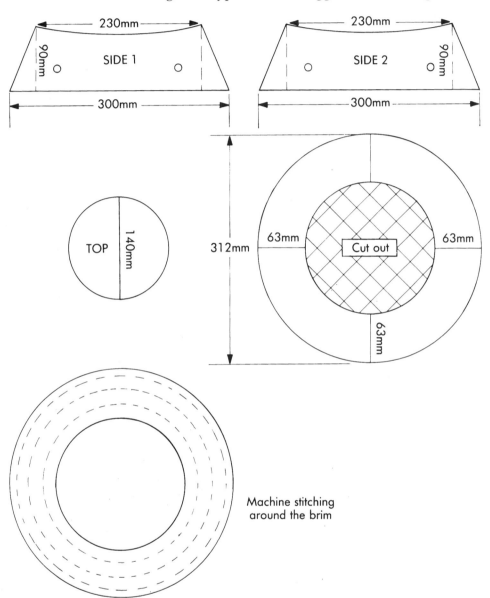

Machine stitching around the brim

Convert these scale drawings into actual patterns and make your own sunhat. If you prepared your own detailed patterns in the earlier assignment you could use them instead if you wish.

A sample answer

You should have made a sunhat which you can wear without embarrassment! In the process of production you should have revealed certain **skills:**

– adopting procedures to reduce waste
– making things accurately
– working with others
– choosing and using appropriate tools
– dealing with unforeseen difficulties

Identify stages and incorporate these into a simple plan

Planning will have been done by you. You should have worked out the **equipment** needed and arranged to borrow what you do not have. The correct sequence of events would have to be sorted out. It is probably best to start from the top, cutting out the pieces and then pinning them together.

The pinned sunhat should be tried on carefully to see if any adjustments are necessary before machining starts. The two pieces which are sewn together to form the brim should probably be machined before the brim is fixed to the other parts.

Use model to assist in making

Work safely

The scissors used should be sharp. However, they need to be used safely, as do the pins. You are allowed one minor pin-prick as a warning!

You should use a machine rather than handsewing. However, you probably needed some help and advice from parent, friend or teacher on how to operate the machine.

Demonstrate by choice and use of equipment an understanding of the principles upon which they work

Estimate cost

You probably managed to buy the necessary pieces of calico (cotton) cheaply from an oddments or remnants counter in a local soft furnishings store, or from a market stall. Thus the overall **cost** would be less than £1.00, assuming that you do not charge yourself for making the sunhat!

Apply knowledge to overcome problems

You may have found the specification inaccurate or the machining instructions too vague. Both of these were done deliberately to test your ability to deal with difficulties.

Now try answering these questions:

1 Why pin pieces together first rather than sewing them straight away?
2 Why use a machine rather than handsewing?
3 Where else could you have tried to get cloth from?

Answers to questions

1 To make sure the pieces fit properly together. Also if you leave pins in when sewing, sewing is easier.
2 The reasons for using a machine rather than handsewing are that it is quicker, more accurate and usually neater and stronger.
3 You could have tried a local dressmaker or market stall; you could have 'scrounged' them from your mother, or even taken apart an old garment and used the cloth.

Making – Level 7

P ROPAGATOR 2

Make the propagator referred to in the assignment on p.106.

The diagrams below show the details for making the propagator suggested in the earlier assignment. You will probably need to read through again the parts list and construction notes. Before starting, you should think ahead to the finished product, **plan** what you are going to do and decide on the **equipment** required.

Components

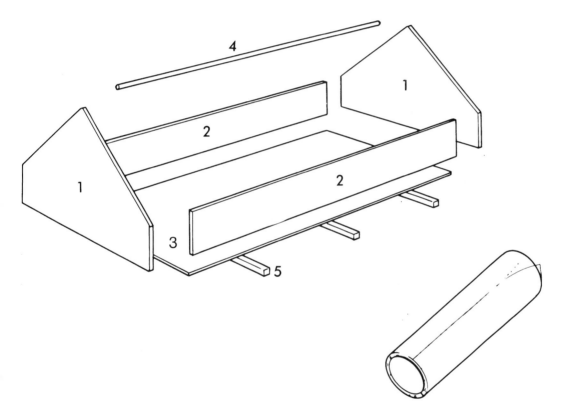

Dimension of end panel

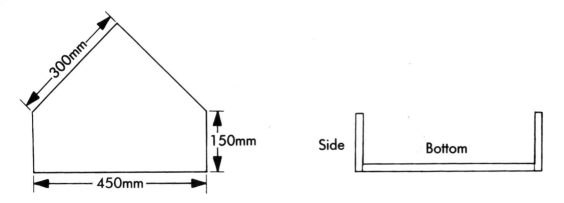

A sample answer

The propagator

It should be a solid and effective structure. During production you could have revealed the following **skills**:

– using your knowledge of the materials
– using the correct processes
– using tools safely and accurately
– overcoming any obstacles which arose
– getting advice when necessary
– interpreting the drawings

Question 1

In making things, **forward planning** is important. You need to gather together all the **pieces** before you start. In this case this probably meant buying wood and screws from a shop and getting permission to use cling film out of the kitchen. The **equipment** also needs to be obtained. Unless someone in your family is a 'handyman' then you might have needed to borrow the relevant saw, or used **school equipment,** e.g. a vice.

Question 2

The specification did not mention the **finish**. You could have painted the wood. If so, the best time is usually at the start, before construction. You also need to decide on a **lining**. One good cheap possibility is bin-liner plastic.

Plan to overcome problems

The specification did not mention **joints**. There are at least six ways to make corners (e.g. 'L' joints) but all you need is something simple and strong. Don't forget the corners will be covered up anyway. A triangular block could be used to get a neat inside corner.

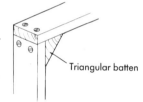
Triangular batten

Competence in making

Tips when making
When using **standard hardboard:**
1 Make sure the rough side is out of view (in this case inside).
2 Use a fine-toothed (tenon) saw to cut with.
3 **Glue** to inside surface if possible.
4 Fit screws *through* hardboard, not into it, if possible.

Right   Wrong

When **fixing screws:**
1 Mark screw positions with intersecting lines, as shown.
2 Drill holes the same diameter as the screw shank.
3 When joining two pieces together, lay the underpiece in position and use a bradawl (see glossary on page 175) through the holes made in the top-piece to mark the underpiece for thread holes.

Carry out working procedures in order to overcome problems

Now try answering these questions:

1 What could you use before painting?
2 Why is a lining needed? What could be used?

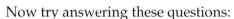

Answers to question 4 (on page 107)

No. Before starting work on making consider:
– a surface finish (perhaps the material will need protecting from the weather)
– a lining
– joints

Answers to questions

1 You could have used a primer on the surface before painting.
2 To prevent water seeping through the joints, e.g. polythene.

Making – Level 6

S POOKY PIZZA

Hallowe'en is the last day of October and it is a time for making spooky things and dressing up. Things like pumpkin lanterns, witches' hats and ghostly cloaks are made because the day is associated with superstition and the supernatural. In this exercise you are going to make some food for the evening.

Below is an example of a simple pizza recipe. You should be able to make the pizza, or something very similar.

Stage 1 – obtain a 550 g packet mix of bread dough, follow the instructions and make the dough. Divide the dough into 12 pieces and roll each out into about a 12 cm circle.

Stage 2 – collect two baking trays big enough to hold the 12 pieces. Slightly smear the surface of the trays with butter.

Stage 3 – spread some sauce, such as tomato, fruity or brown, onto the dough. Lightly fry a few onions and place them on top. You will need fat for the frying pan. You could sprinkle some seasoning over each pizza base.

Stage 4 – cut some cheese into thin slices and place the slices on top of your pizza. You could even make a ghostly face shape by cutting up pieces of pepper and arranging them on the cheese!

Stage 5 – bake the pizzas for 15 to 20 minutes at one of the following temperatures – gas mark 6, or 200° C or 400° F. They will be ready to eat once baked.

You do not have to make the pizza on Hallowe'en or in such quantity! It might be better to experiment with a smaller amount first. Although the theme in this assignment is Hallowe'en you can make the pizza at any time and on any occasion. You may wish to vary the shape or the face idea as appropriate.

Before you start, make sure that you have:

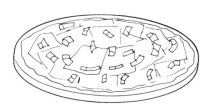

– all the necessary ingredients
– the correct equipment
– clean work surfaces
– a detailed knowledge of what you want to do
– enough time from start to finish (allow an hour?)
– permission from parents to do it
– enough willing 'guinea pigs' to eat what is made!

Don't forget to clear away afterwards.
Don't forget to wash and dry up!

Information technology – Level 3

F AST FOOD

Carry out a survey of fast food take-aways in your area.

This information needs collecting, storing and then retrieving (i.e. feeding into the computer and then taking out the information that you need). Thus, you will need to be able to use a data base. You are not expected to be able to structure one for yourself but you should be able to enter the data.

A good structure for the sort of data base you will need is shown below. It contains four fields (i.e. types of information collected). Use it as the basis for your survey. However, you will need to prepare your own data base from your survey. There is general guidance on how to do this on pages 90 to 94.

NAME   STREET   TYPE   FOOD

Remember, you must collect information in an organized way. Because of this, it might be a good idea to devise a code of abbreviations. For example:

T = take-away

R = restaurant

B = both

A sample answer

The data base below is not perfect but it does do what is required.

NAME	STREET	TYPE	FOOD
Ernie Becket	Market St	T,B	fc
Green Star Fish	Nicholson St	T	fc
J. Sutherland	St Peters Ave	T	fc
Agrah Indian	Sea View St	R	i
Bella Pizza	Market Sq	T	p
Hobson's	Grimsby Rd	R	v
Inn on the Park	Blundell Park	R	v
The Seaway	Alexandria Road	B	v

The information has been recorded in the four categories. Suitable abbreviations have been used. You should be able to work out the food code quite easily ('V' stands for 'various foods provided').

From the data you can see which restaurants and take-aways serve which food and where they are located.

NAME	STREET	TYPE	FOOD
Ernie Becket	Market St	T,B	fc
Green Star Fish	Nicholson St	T	fc
J. Sutherland	St Peters Ave	T	fc
Bella Pizza	Market Sq	T	p

This printout shows the selection of information from the data base. It has been searched for take-aways (T) and four have been retrieved.

This printout shows only one type of food sold. As you can see, there are only three of the eight premises which sell a variety of foods (V).

NAME	STREET	TYPE	FOOD
Hobson's	Grimsby Rd	R	v
Inn on the Park	Blundell Park	R	v
The Seaway	Alexandria Road	B	v

Now answer these questions:

1 What do you think are the main weaknesses of this data base?
2 Taking the two extracts together what do you think they will tell you?

Answers to questions

1 Only a very small number of take-aways have been considered. However, there *are* many more in the area surveyed (Cleethorpes) because it is a holiday resort. In a small town, on the other hand, for example, eight, might be a reasonable number. So the number in your survey will depend upon where you live.

2 One conclusion which you could reach might be that there is a gap in this market for a take-away selling a wide **variety** of fast foods.

Information technology – Level 4

S PREADSHEETS

There are usually differences in price when the same item is bought from different shops. Below is some data collected on 10 items of household expenditure which shows this. The figures are in pounds and pence.

The product	Shop A	Shop B	Shop C
Heinz vegetable soup 800 g	0.50	0.58	
Large white loaf	0.64	0.62	
2 kg Vitalite margarine	2.64	2.60	
1 dozen eggs	1.30	1.20	
Fussell's condensed milk	0.64	0.78	
1 kg sugar	0.49	0.56	
1 pint milk	0.32	0.32	
KP crisps – 21 assorted	2.30	2.70	
500 g tomatoes	0.60	0.51	
1 pack (7) Penguins	0.50	0.60	

1 Collect relevant information from a third shop (shop C).
2 Choose an appropriate software package to store and retrieve the information for all three shops.
3 Devise a spreadsheet for this information.
4 Calculate on the computer which shop offers the cheapest shopping and which shop is the dearest.
5 Apply a 10 per cent price increase to shop A. You could do this on your spreadsheet by instructing the computer using an appropriate formula.

Have you compared like with like when collecting the information?
Why might there be price differences?
Read in Chapter 3 about spreadsheets.
What formulae do you need for the calculations?

If you do not have access to a computer this exercise can still be done by writing out your own spreadsheet and using a calculator for the calculations.

Information technology – Level 6

COMPANY LOGOS

Logos are important to companies. This is because they enable consumers to identify the company at a glance. Logos are often simple signs which are displayed on company products, brochures, advertising, etc. However, these signs are often very effective at sending powerful messages to customers.

BP, the petrol company, decided to change their image for the 1990s. However, they wished to retain a similar visual style to their previous 1930s and 1958 logos. This was because BP's research showed that, in the eyes of their customers, the BP shield symbolized excellence and integrity.

The 1990 logo which BP came up with is very simple. There is a background colour which is green. The BP shield, which is yellow, has the letters inside. It is illustrated below.

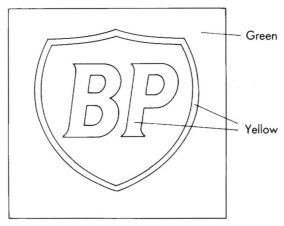

Your task is to produce a new logo. This could be for a company or for your school. The logo needs to be presented to an audience using computer graphics and text. You should select appropriate software for the graphics in order to produce the logo. You should be able also to outline your reasoning behind the logo using words. You could combine the graphics and text on one page.

Look at existing logos and consider what you think makes them successful. The BP logo, for example, is worth attention because of its simplicity.
What images are conveyed in the logos?
What images do you wish to suggest in your logo?
Will you use a picture, shape or symbol?
Are letters, initials or words needed?
What colours will be used? Is a contrast required?
Are different shapes relevant?
Will you need lines, borders, etc. in your layout?
Will you want a background colour, picture or image?

L ONGER ASSIGNMENTS

These assignments you will find more wide ranging than the ones you have tackled so far. Each assignment demands that you use most of the technology skills. Each begins with a piece of information that serves to stimulate you into action. You should initially think for yourself about what you have to do. If you are still uncertain how to start you might find it useful to go back to Chapter 1 and re-read about the design process.

When you have sorted out an idea for the given task read through the section about identifying needs and opportunities. There you will find guidance and perhaps ideas for opportunities that you may not have already considered. There are no ready-made answers and so in all the assignments only hints and tips have been given.

Before reading the generating a design section you should think about what factors are important. In some cases you have been given a preliminary design exercise to do. You could and should consider the points that are suggested. You will notice that these are much more detailed and thorough than those given in the previous short assignments! This is because they are seeking to test you at a higher level.

When considering planning and making it is advisable to read the appropriate section first. A lot of detailed help has been provided so that you can make a quality product, and in the best way.

In practice, evaluation is done throughout the process as well as at the end. However, this section tries to draw together various thoughts and ideas on how you could have judged your performance and your product.

The information technology aspect is not directly addressed in each assignment, because it is impossible to know what IT is available to you. However, there has been provided an IT element which tells you how information technology could be used. Further guidance and useful information can be found by re-reading Chapter 3: Information Technology.

L ONGER ASSIGNMENT 1: LOCKS AND KEYS

Identifying needs and opportunities

Oak Developments plc,
Peartree Estate,
Crowthorpe,
York,
DN1 52Z

Intro-Design,
Unit 10,
The Works,
Wilson Road,
Swath,
SW2 3PS

5 August 1995

Dear Sirs,

I write to you in connection with a new complex we are building. A major part of this development is the community accommodation for the non- and partially-sighted. This development will be warden attended but the occupants will want to be as independent as possible.

Our purpose in contacting you relates to security. Each occupant will require complete access to all facilities. This includes two external doors, a common room, utility services and of course their own private room. We therefore require a simple and economical key coding system suitable for the non-sighted so that they may enjoy the same privacy and security that sighted people do.

All the locks will be of the same type and your design should include some means by which occupants can easily locate key holes.

At this stage I do not see the need for us to meet as I am sure that you can communicate your design solution on paper. Unfortunately we are already two months behind schedule so a prompt response is essential.

Yours faithfully

R.D Milton
(Project Co-ordinator)

This letter then is your brief. How do you start to come up with a solution?

A good way would be to look at some keys and locks. There are two common types fitted to doors, called 'Yale' and 'mortice'. In the letter the project co-ordinator states that all the locks will be of the same type, although he does not state which. It might be that you find one particular type more suitable than the other. You will therefore need to do some research.

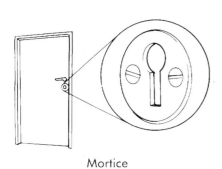

Mortice

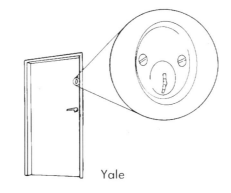

Yale

Your first task is to put yourself in the place of the occupants and try with a bunch of keys to open a door with your eyes closed. This should be in a **safe place**, away from traffic (if outside) and not at the top of a staircase (if inside).

It would be a good idea to get someone to watch you so that they can spot any problems you are having of which you might not be aware.

Write down on your design sheet the two basic aspects of the problem which are:

1 Selecting the appropriate key.
2 Locating the key in the key hole.

1 Selecting the appropriate key

This requires some form of 'code' (a code is a kind of language that communicates information through the use of your senses). Think about your different senses and select the most appropriate. Sight is obviously not one to be considered so which of the others would be best?

How good is your sense of touch?

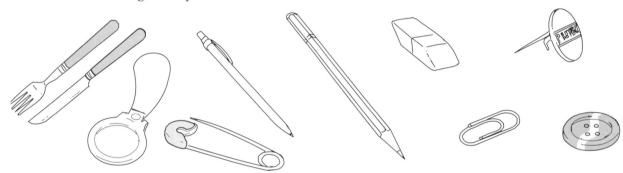

Assemble about ten everyday items (pen, pencil, table knife, fork, and so on) and with your eyes closed try to identify what they are. Ask yourself how you identified the object and how easy it was. A second exercise would be to try to identify a number of different coins, again with your eyes closed or in the dark.

It seems then that when handling objects we can, through our sense of touch, recognize familiar objects. This is done by assessing:

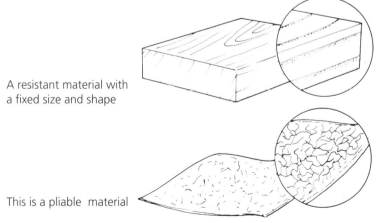

A resistant material with a fixed size and shape

This is a pliable material

MATERIAL CHARACTERISTICS:
Soft/hard, warm/cold, rigid/malleable
e.g. wood, leather, metal and plastic

SHAPE AND FORM:
Regular/irregular, e.g. flat or rounded

SIZE:
Large, medium or small

TEXTURE (surface pattern):
e.g. rough or smooth

These characteristics may be a key to developing an identification code.

Generating a design

Now look at a bunch of keys to see what they have in common. There are of course a number of qualities and properties they share. The one you should be interested in is the hole at the twist grip end, by which the keys can be attached to other objects. Consider this and the information gained from the previous page. This may give you an idea that links certain aspects of the problem together. If you are still not sure then turn to page 132.

The next stage is to develop some prototypes. This is an important step in production. In the motor industry, for example, there are always a few cars made up by hand before the design is finalized and the cars made on the production line. This is because if there are mistakes in the design they are easier to spot and to correct or modify. It also allows for last-minute changes.

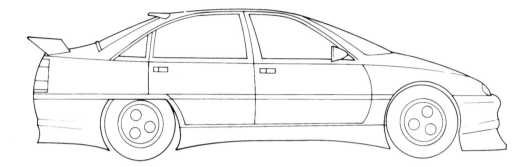

A prototype design for a car

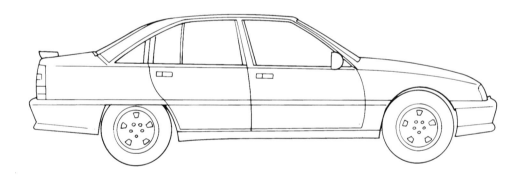

The finished model

On your design sheet you could draw around some keys with a pencil (using the keys as a template), adding your ideas to these outlines (perhaps in colour) afterwards.

Planning and making

One of the most important aspects of this stage is evaluating the prototypes. Three of the points you will have to consider are:

1 The number of keys you have to code, and the possibility of having to expand the system to include more keys.
2 The most suitable production material.
3 The time it would take to work the material.
  What do you think are the other three important aspects to consider?
4 ....
  ....
  ....
5 ....
  ....
  ....

6 ....
....
....

Check your points against those listed below. You should now be able to decide what material you intend to use. Remember that you are only producing a proto-type, so even if you want the final product in stainless steel you should choose a material now which is easy to work, cheap and for which you have the tools. This is exactly how it happens in industry! Transferring your design onto your chosen final materials could perhaps be made easier by tracing or by using templates.

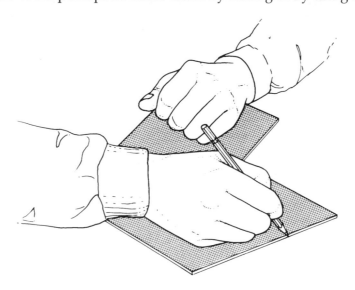

Aspects to consider

Apart from the points listed earlier in this assignment you should check the points you have considered against those listed below.

Material Considerations:	Cost
	Available sizes
	Supply
	Construction processes
	Durability
	Strength
Time Considerations:	That necessary to make one
	That necessary for mass production
Functional Considerations:	Size
	Weight
	Comfort
Aesthetic Considerations:	Visual appearance
	Colours
	How things feel
Safety Considerations:	Sharp edges
	Pointed shapes
	The use of non-toxic paints
Security Considerations:	Loss of keys from ring
	Loss of keys breaching security

Evaluating

You need to judge the system you have designed and produced 'objectively': look for the good points and the bad points. This could be done by assessing your solution according to the checklist on page 135. Also, it might be wise to get someone else's opinion about what you have produced. Ideally a blind person would be best. However, you could get a friend or a parent to pretend to be blind in order to test your system in practice. This would enable you to consider the viewpoint of the user. After this testing you might think of additional improvements you could make. If this proves to be the case, make a note of them and think about how they could be incorporated in your design. Similarly you need to think about alternative materials (ones which you might not have access to) but which might be cheaper to buy and work with.

In your final evaluation you would have to look closely at production costs for this would give you some idea about what producers might want to charge for it. Making a one-off is very different from 'tooling up' for mass production. You are not in a position to consider how to go about mass production but you can ask yourself how you could have made it quicker, on a larger scale and if you have used the best tools. Apart from the cost of raw materials other factors which influence production costs are the amount of material wasted, the number of different processes involved, packaging and the producing of the instruction leaflet.

Finally your answer to this particular project should be presented in a way that addresses the request of the original letter. Successful designers are those who answer the questions and problems put to them. If you have enjoyed solving this problem and have produced an original idea talk to somebody about it. There may be a gap in the market.

2 Locating the key in the key hole

The second half of this problem is easier than the first. Many blind people are able to locate the key in the key hole without any help. However, a little thought about this problem could make some people's lives much easier.

Think back to your initial investigation when, with your eyes closed, you tried to unlock a door. The chances are in an attempt to find the key hole you ran your hand over the door in a number of sweeping movements until you came in contact with the key hole. If by chance you ran your hand over the edge of the door you would have been able to use the gap between door and frame to home in on the key hole. Perhaps this might be something you could use.

Generating a design

Again thinking back to your sense of touch activities you should have been able to differentiate between different textured surfaces. Given that doors are smooth, applying a contrasting texture in a specific way could indicate the direction of the key hole.

Planning and making

Textures can be incised (carved into a surface) or embossed (applied onto a surface), see next page. The problem is coming up with a solution that works and at the same time is visually acceptable. After all a texture that has been applied in a slapdash way could give the appearance that the doors had been vandalized!

Incised

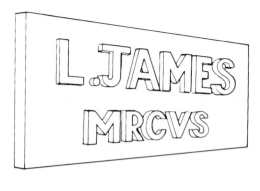

Embossed

Evaluating

Any modifications to the doors depends partly on your solution to the coding system. It may also be affected by your choice of lock (Yale or mortice).

Another general factor to consider is the appearance of your design solution. Although the appearance of the door does not much affect a blind person you need to bear in mind the fact that sighted people will also use the building. Thus a modified door and/or lock needs to blend in with the environment of the building.

Again cost considerations need to be examined. Usually modifications to existing systems and products are cheaper than brand new ones. A solution which causes a minimum amount of modification will probably be preferable. However, you could propose two possible solutions – one for a low budget modification and another for a new installation which might be low cost if installed during the building process. The latter is perhaps more appropriate in this case.

A fundamentally important factor is **safety**. For instance, a protruding edge might not be dangerous for a sighted person but it could be hazardous for a non-sighted one. You should also consider fire and the need to evacuate the building quickly. Access from the outside should of course require a key at all times but it is essential that a quick exit be possible without the use of any keys at all. This will require the use of a special type of lock.

Apart from personal safety, there is, of course, also the issue of protecting personal property to consider.

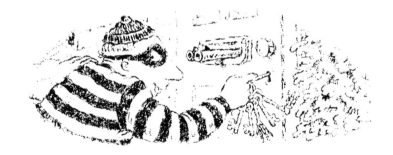

CHECKLIST

The illustrations below show a number of possible solutions to the key coding problem. Although each of the ideas has some good points none of them is an example of particularly good design.

Consider each idea in turn together with the notes below, then assess them under the following headings:

Ease of Production :	simple/involved
Cost of Production :	low/high
Coding System :	simple/elaborate
Adaptability :	Yale/mortice
Ease of Handling :	light/heavy
	tangle-free/liable to tangle
	small and comfortable/big and bulky
Durability :	liable to break or wear/trouble free

Solution A Each key would have a different number of lengths of string attached to it.

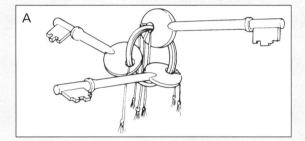

Solution B Here the keys are held together by different shaped key rings.

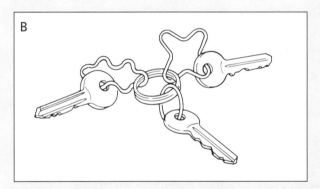

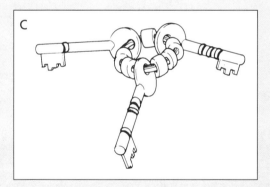

Solution C Keys are separated by different numbers of beads. The idea is backed-up by a second coding system of a different number of rings appearing on the shaft of each key.

List only the weak aspects of each design

	Solution A	**Solution B**	**Solution C**
Ease of production			
Cost of production			
Coding system			
Adaptability			
Ease of handling			
Durability			

Now think of the opposite to the answers you have just given and this will help you to find the strong aspects of key design which you can then incorporate into your own ideas!

INFORMATION TECHNOLOGY

Using a computer on the first half of this problem would not be very helpful. However the second aspect of the task (designing an aid to locate the key hole) may benefit from the use of this technology. Art graphics packages could be used to produce an image of a plain door. This image could then be used each time you wanted to develop a different design. If no computer is available the drawn image could be reproduced by using a photocopier.

L ONGER ASSIGNMENT 2: PARTY PIECE

This is one of over 250 free invitations to Hi-Tech's grand opening. If you receive one, have you got the pluck to design and wear some 'hi-tech' attire?

Hi-Tech to compete in our High Street

Jenny Armid gives us the background on business in the High Street. As some novel invitations drop through our letterboxes she explains what other tactics we can expect to see.

There are many ways in which High Street retailers compete and judging by the number of empty shops in our main shopping street, many are unsuccessful.

So, as a former motorists' discount centre prepares to open its doors as 'Hi-Tech', an electrical retailer, how will Hi-Tech compete for our trade and what can we expect to happen?

Prices

The main type of competition will, not surprisingly, be by price. For example, a firm such as Hi-Tech entering a new market may use a low price to get a foothold. This is known as a penetration price. Asda did this in food retailing on a wide range of goods and as result it is now established as one of the five biggest groups in Britain.

Can we expect to see a price war in our High Street?

A similar trick used by most big retailers is the 'loss leader'. This is where a product is sold at a price equal to (or below) its cost, so firms do not make a profit by selling it. However, it attracts the customers in.

'Gimmicks'

Another pricing strategy is to use sale promotion 'gimmicks' which makes goods seem cheaper. Examples of this are special offers. There is just such an offer ('£20 if you trade in your old cooker') on at the moment in the High Street. Discount vouchers ('£10 off next purchase') and free gifts ('Buy two and get one free') are similar 'gimmicks'. Hi-Tech's fancy dress prizes are like the free gifts type of sales promotion. Another popular 'gimmick' is 'Interest free credit'. This is now very common, particularly on electrical hardware so I'm sure we can expect to see this facility offered to us.

Quality

Most shops like to think that they sell quality products (most of us like to think we buy

them). However, it is not that simple. A firm needs to decide which part of the market to aim for. It could choose to be 'up market' which means that high quality and expensive goods are sold. The name 'Hi-Tech' suggests an 'up market' store. The advertising that we are about to see will therefore be matched carefully to this image, appealing particularly to certain customers. We will therefore be able to judge their success by the number of BMWs and XR3is we see in the car park. Skodas, Ladas and 2CVs might mean they have got it wrong! A recent success of 'targeting' has been seen in food retailing where Sainsburys have pushed a 'green image', stressing how environmentally friendly many of their products are.

Brands

Brands are used to distinguish one company's products from another's. Hi-Tech have popular label names as well as their own Hi-Tech label products, which are sold at lower prices. About 40 per cent of supermarket sales are 'own label goods'. A good brand name should be:

– short
– easy to pronounce
– descriptive of the goods
– original

How then do we rate Hi-Tech? Brands are supported by packaging which is designed to sell the goods as well as protect the goods. Packaging encourages 'impulse buying'. Thus we are encouraged to buy goods because they look good! Sometimes, however, firms can be rather more successful than they intended. Shell state that their most valued asset is not any of their oil reserves or technological secrets but in fact their company logo, the shell. When Coca-Cola put the curved stripe under their name sales went through the roof. These two examples prove the power of product identity and show just how unpredictable we can be when it comes to spending money.

Hi-Tech in our High Street? I rate their chances quite high but as some of you know I've painted flowers on my BMW!

Identifying needs and opportunities

The task therefore is to produce some kind of personal attire which is based on and promotes technological hardware. At the end of this exercise not only will you have increased your understanding of technology but you should have produced an attractive costume piece which you might wish to wear! Perhaps this could be the theme for a fancy dress party to which you might invite all your friends.

The first thing you must do is make sure you understand the terms correctly. You need to get some idea about technological hardware. This means the kind of products offered for sale by such a superstore. These firms put a lot of effort into advertising their products through demonstrations, sales, free newspapers and instant credit. Newspapers and magazines also contain masses of pictorial information about a wide variety of electrical goods.

The statement 'appropriate dress' may not be quite so easy to understand. A few years ago people would have taken it to mean 'fancy dress' in its most obvious form. Of course it still can mean that. However, it can now mean rather more. You could, for example, design a mask for the occasion. Alternatively, you could design a collection of unisex costume jewellery. Make-up could also be used to great effect. The important thing is to think very broadly (that means include as many ideas as possible) and since the invitation is for two it is suggested that you work on this one with a friend. This is a good way of coming up with even more interesting ideas.

Early evaluating

Having got some ideas about the kind of item(s) you would like to produce, rather than launching straight into production, it is probably best that you go out and see if the idea is already on the market. There's not a lot of point in trying to make something that already exists. You may know of a shop that hires fancy dress costumes or one that sells novelty jewellery. There must also be 'high-tech' industries, such as computer software houses, that promote their products by having pictures and logos printed as T-shirt designs.

If you do find an article which you think fits the requirements assess how successful it is. Ask yourself the questions shown in the list below.

Questions	Yes	No	Comments
Is it in keeping with a 'high-tech' image? Does it promote electrical hardware? Is it distinctive? Is it attractive? Is it well made? Would it suit me? Is it good value for money? Dare I wear it? Would I buy it? Would it win a competition? Would it need anything else to go with it? Is there anything else that would go with it?			

The last question is to do with originality and raises the point that in buying a mass-produced article (to buy an original or 'one-off' would be very expensive) you run the risk of being seen in the same article as somebody else! This would kill your chances of winning a prize. However that's not to say that items could not be adapted and 'customized'.

If eventually you are not able to find anything appropriate to wear at the Hi-Tech opening then this means that at least you have found a gap in the market. And if you have found something you might not be able to wear it but at least it might trigger lots of your own ideas.

Generating a design

You can tackle this stage in one of two ways.

1 Below is a chart where the two aspects of the problem are cross-referenced.

You can read down or across depending on what you want to make and the way you are thinking. If, for example, you want to make a mask then follow that line across considering all the options from a complete electrical appliance such as a hair dryer right through to an abstract pattern derived from observation, for example, one based on diodes and transistors. Doing this should give you various design ideas for your mask. On the other hand you might have found some electrical components which interest you and you don't mind the pattern dictating the party piece you are going to wear. If this is the case then look down that column and consider each of the products in turn. The blank spaces are for you to fill in your ideas.

What I have observed in order to gain ideas				
What I want to wear	Complete electrical appliance	Part of electrical appliance	Components	Patterns derived from observation
Complete costume				
Mask				
Jewellery				
Customization of already existing outfits and clothes				

2 As an alternative to this approach you could develop your ideas by studying specific objects themselves. This is rather like artists trying to gain inspiration! It might be, for example, that after studying part of a printed circuit board (PCB) you come up with a good design for a T-shirt.

Whichever way you choose to work you will need to look in detail at the objects in question. If you are considering complete electrical appliances then you could use those in your own home. You should however make sure you have permission to do so. If looking at these objects involves handling them then you must make sure that doing so will not damage them and that they are switched off and disconnected from the mains. You must be careful when using equipment like a camera, for example, because it can very easily be damaged if fiddled with or if left in the sun.

If you are thinking that you might want to work from a small scale concentrating on components such as micro-chips and transistors then you will need to get hold of some. You could of course go to an appropriate shop: the very new type where everything comes in its own bubble or blister pack or the old-fashioned type which is usually stacked to the ceiling with abandoned televisions! This second type of shop might actually be your best bet for you may be able to obtain some defective or obsolete parts which are of no practical use but which could be very useful to you. You may of course have your own supply of defective or unwanted electrical goods. Permission to dismantle them is the first thing you need to obtain, closely followed by ensuring that they are disconnected from the mains and that they have not been switched on for a long time (some devices can hold an electrical charge for a very long time). **Old televisions should not be taken to pieces.**

Presume then that you have some source material such as a printed circuit board (PCB). Consider how you can extract the design information needed. If you are thinking about developing patterns then it might be a good idea to use a viewfinder as shown on the next page (also see page 142). This will not only help you select the most interesting area but it will also help you to see a pattern. A viewfinder would also be useful if you wanted to concentrate on individual components such as diodes and transistors. Components such as these could perhaps be modelled on a large scale and used to make jewellery.

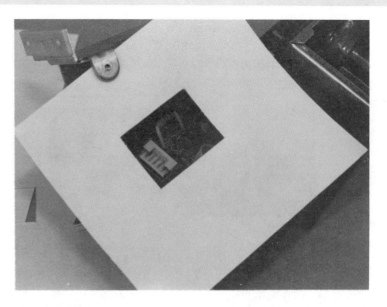

Planning and making

In order to encourage you to develop your own ideas this project has been made very open-ended. This means detailed advice cannot be given at this stage. However, there follow a few suggestions.

If you take the mask idea you could of course design your own shape but why not think about buying a simple mask from a shop, or using the case from an old hair dryer or cassette player? You could spray it a different colour and then decorate it with electronic components. Other features could be added as desired. You might be able to use different coloured light emitting diodes known as LEDs (tiny light bulbs) which could be wired into a simple circuit and powered by a very small battery (see 'electronics' on page 142). Features could then be illuminated. Wire or cassette tape could be used for hair. Masks are usually designed to cover up faces but you could think about designing masks for other parts of the body. There are all sorts of possibilities for robots and androids.

Fabric paints are very popular at the moment and are a good way of producing coloured designs straight onto clothes. Other ways include sewing on different coloured or patterned materials.

Giant electronic components could be made in a variety of modelling materials although you need to think about the weight. Small cylinders can be produced easily from strips of paper dipped in glue and rolled up tightly. They could then be painted and either added to existing jewellery or developed into individual pieces.

Evaluating

In the earlier evaluation you considered existing fancy dress costumes and/or novelty jewellery in some detail. Now you need to assess what you have made or modified in response to this challenge.

It is difficult for you to judge your design fairly because you are likely to think it is a good one. However, you could ask a parent, a relative or a friend what they think about your technological attire. It is probably worth explaining briefly the background to your design so that people can judge how appropriate it is.

You might have been limited in your design by a lack of available components or materials. However, it does not matter as long as you did realize that there could have been other solutions to the problem. For example, you might have bought a cheap mask which proved not to be as durable as you wanted and this seriously hampered your ideal solution to the problem. It is always important to consider qualities such as strength, comfort, finish and visual appearance.

The way you went about design and making also requires assessment by you. Did you undertake any tests or build a prototype first? It may be that you were hampered by lack of equipment. Again this is not too important as long as you at least recognize what is needed to produce a better artefact.

In considering the best way to make this article you should have thought about speed, accuracy and reliability. Ask yourself if you worked safely and with little waste.

Cost is always an important element in any project. In this assignment you were not given a budget to keep to. However, you should have viewed your creation as a 'low-tech' solution to a design problem. You were probably able to get the necessary items at little cost.

It is important to realize that often the biggest cost is not the cost of the materials. The time taken to make a product can be expensive. The cost of this time depends upon how much you charge an hour! You may have produced something which you think could be sold commercially at a profit but it needs to be borne in mind that in the business world all costs have to be considered, including heating, lighting and business rates.

A final factor, and one which it is difficult to measure but which it is hoped is high, is the pleasure you have derived from producing your 'appropriate dress'.

Viewfinders

These are very simple but effective tools which, as the name implies, help in the selection and composition of views. Viewfinders do this by covering up what you don't wish to see thereby focusing your attention on the selected area. You are then able to appreciate graphic qualities such as pattern and shape much more easily (look again at page 140).

All you need to produce a viewfinder is a thin piece of card from which you cut a regular-shaped hole. This hole needs to be in the middle of the card and to be in the same proportion as the design you wish to produce. You then pass the viewfinder over the surface of the object(s) you are looking at, moving the card around slowly while looking through the hole. Once you have found an interesting view you can use a piece of sticky tape or Blu-Tack to hold the viewfinder in position. Sometimes it is best to try cards with different-sized holes in order to create the best design.

Electronics

Electrical circuit diagrams

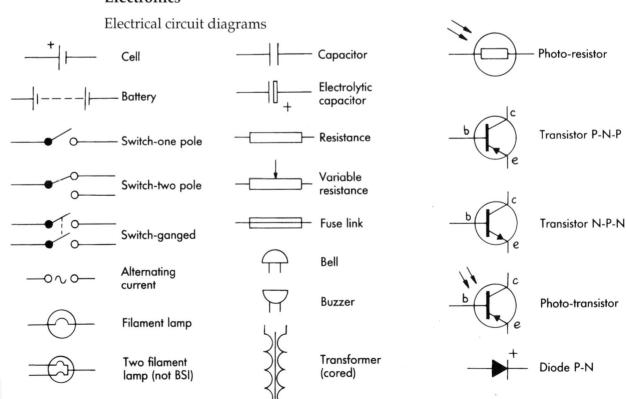

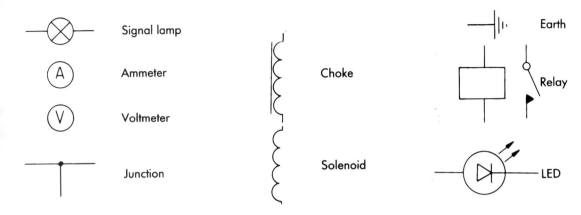

Signal lamp

Ammeter

Voltmeter

Junction

Choke

Solenoid

Earth

Relay

LED

Don't worry if you don't understand all these symbols. Their value to you is as pictures which you can identify.

Reproduced below are some electronic circuits which would cause LEDs to flash on and off. On a very simple level this information could be used to create patterns of the type you might be seeking.

If you decide that you want to make these circuits up then the wires could be fixed together by twisting them together using a pair of pliers and then taping over the joint. A more permanent method would be to solder the joints (after first testing the circuit) but this would require special tools and you may need assistance from a skilled adult.

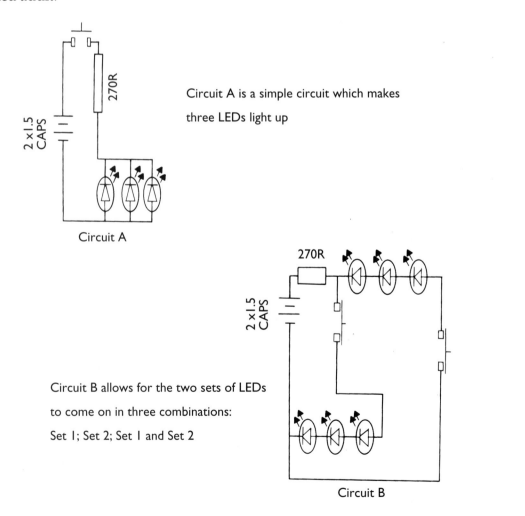

Circuit A is a simple circuit which makes

three LEDs light up

Circuit A

Circuit B allows for the two sets of LEDs

to come on in three combinations:

Set 1; Set 2; Set 1 and Set 2

Circuit B

L ONGER ASSIGNMENT 3: PHONE CARD

STELAPHONE SYSTEMS LTD

announce a **DESIGN COMPETITION**

for an INFORMATION/PHONE CARD

This new international information system will be available next spring. All types of information will be available through the phone card system as well as the ordinary use of Stelaphone communication systems. To mark the launch of this new superior system Stelaphone invite design entries for this new type of phone card system.

The company requires the card to:

1 Operate through standard credit/phone card technology. This means that the card should be the same size, shape and weight as those in use at the present.
2 Be easy to use for both able- and non-able-bodied persons.
3 Have some means of indicating the number of unused units.
4 Have a user-identity function. This means that the person who presents the card can be recognized as the rightful owner, usually by a signature or secret code.
5 Have a counterfeit protection logo. This is a company symbol that is very difficult or expensive to copy – a hologram, for example.
6 Be attractive and distinctive in appearance.
7 Bear the company logo.
8 Avoid the problem of being discarded after use.

Up to three entries may be submitted for the proposed denominations of 10, 50 and 100 unit cards.

YOU COULD WIN:

FIRST PRIZE – A 14 day trip for two to America staying in luxury hotels, and as VIP guests of Stelaphone visiting a host of holiday attractions including Stelaphone's new International Communications Centre in Florida. $2000 spending money is included!

SECOND PRIZE – A 14 day holiday for two in London, again staying in luxury accommodation and having a wide range of activities to enjoy. Included in this prize is £1000 spending money!

THIRD PRIZE – 5 years' free subscription to Stelaphone's Information Systems including all installation costs!

RULES:

Entries should be on card and attached to an official entry form.

Closing date for this competition is Jan. 31 next year.

Winning entries will become the sole property of Stelaphone International.

The judges' decision will be final.

No correspondence will be entered into.

Employees of Stelaphone International are not eligible for entry.

Winners will be notified by post and results published in the national press.

Please cut here ···

Stelaphone International Competition Entry Form

NAME... **ADDRESS**...

....

SPECIFICATIONS ....

....

....

Indentifying needs and opportunities

At first sight this assignment might seem rather difficult but working to the design formula of identifying needs and opportunities, generating a design, planning and making, and evaluating, these should help you to break the problem down into smaller, more manageable sections.

The first task therefore is to 'identify needs'. In this case this has already been done for you. The requirements of the phone card are stated clearly in the details of the competition. However, the way you consider the points may help you come up with some ideas. Another valuable lesson is to learn 'not to rediscover the wheel', in other words don't start from scratch. Instead, ask your older relatives if you can look at some of their 'plastic' (credit cards and so on). You must understand however that credit and cash cards are very valuable items and under no circumstances should you look at them without permission or, worse, leave them lying around. Spent phone cards on the other hand are easier to acquire. Have a look inside a normally busy phone card booth and you will see why Stelaphone don't want their image spoilt by a similar litter problem!

Generating a design

Let's presume then that you are able to consider the competition brief with some out-of-date credit cards or spent phone cards in front of you. Consider each point in turn and see how successfully the problems have been resolved by the original designers. Consider also how easy it would be for the card to be loaded into an appropriate machine in the dark and while wearing gloves. Each card will have good and bad features. It may prove helpful therefore if you write these points down on your design sheet using the list of design specifications shown on the competition poster.

Another step forward might be, after you have considered each point in turn, to look at them again, but this time in 'groups'. This way you might find you are able to meet two or more of the specifications with one idea. Some features of the specification have been grouped below. Consider if the groups used are helpful. If not, re-group them!

1 Operate through standard credit/
phone card technology

8 Avoid the problem of being
discarded after use

} This grouping doesn't help

5 Have a counterfeit protection logo

7 Bear the company logo

} These could become one task

You may have decided that some tasks should be linked, such as 5 and 7. On the other hand, you may decide that it would be better to link 8, 7 and 6. At this stage there is perhaps no right answer, it depends on how your thoughts and ideas are developing.

Below are some points you may wish to consider. You should not try to use them all, only the ones that fit into your ideas or scheme of thoughts. You could:

1 Use an old card as a template when drawing up your ideas.

2 Try to see some cards in use. Notice how some cards are put in the machine end first while others are designed to work on their broad side. Notice also that some cards disappear totally inside the machine while other systems leave one edge or side sticking out. Could this allow you to redesign one edge?

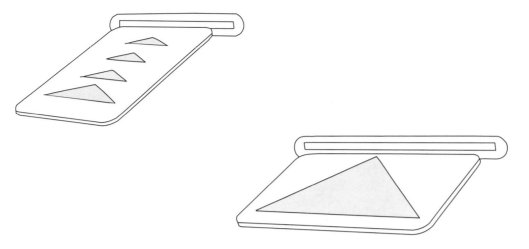

3 Design the card so it is completely smooth. However, some credit cards have some details embossed (raised above the surface). Could this help the blind and the partially-sighted?

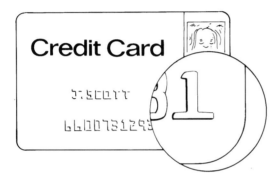

4 Decide to show the remaining value (number of unused units) by specifying a means of cutting or grinding notches on the side. Alternatively colours could change or patterns could disappear.
5 Decide that the security device be based on signatures or a secret code, or perhaps some other system altogether.
6 Look at some £5 or £10 notes to see how the Bank of England has guarded against forgery. Holograms perform a similar function on some credit cards.
7 Try to solve the litter problem by recommending some form of refund on spent cards. Unfortunately such systems are expensive to administer. Can you think of any other ways?

With luck these ideas have caused you to think and develop some ideas of your own. If this is the case then you are ready to move on to the next stage. If not turn to page 150 where there are some entries to the competition for you to look at and make comments on.

When you are ready to develop your own ideas start by looking again at the section on design sheets on pages 14 to 16. Then gather all the information together and spend a few minutes considering it. Tackle the points in your own order and when you have completed all of them combine the best solutions together to form a completed design. Don't spend too much time on detailed drawing; instead produce simple drawings, saving your time in order to make a really good job of the final design. If you have several good ideas don't discard them, instead develop them into an alternative solution. Remember – the competition allows for up to three entries!

Planning and making

One of the conditions of entry is that the ideas have to be submitted on card. This could be achieved in two ways: by drawing pictures of your completed designs onto one piece of card, or by making and presenting the phone cards as actual objects. Since this book is about 'learning by doing' it is hoped that you will want to make your idea.

Success at this stage is about making the card as realistic as possible. Felt and fibre-tipped pens will be useful for the colour while a convincing shiny effect could be achieved by covering your products with the sticky-backed plastic often used on books. As an alternative think about the material used in kitchens to cover up food. Aluminium foil can be used to represent a hologram.

Evaluating

The process of evaluation has been going on as you have considered and reconsidered the problem and your own ideas. It might be a good idea to consider the evaluation under two headings:

1 Technical.
2 Marketing.

1 Technical
This means ensuring the finished product meets the specification and performs as the company would wish.

You may have already done some evaluating, if as suggested in generating a design, you looked at page 150 and judged the four entries. If you did not, turn to that page and consider these entries now.

You can compare these entries with your own phone card. In order to judge the good points of the different entries you need to decide, as the judges will, the following:

• Which of the eight points in the specification is most important?
• Which of the eight points in the specification is least important?
• How well are the different points met?

Initially you might have considered how the machine which receives the card works; this could give clues to design. So might your consideration of the surface of the card: it might not necessarily be flat or plain. And the existence of holes, a bar code or a scratch surface are all possible ways of metering the number of unused units.

INFORMATION TECHNOLOGY

Art/graphics

Here an art package could be very useful. Text and symbols could be moved around in many different combinations offering all sorts of possibilities. When you do arrive at a final design the same image could be used to produce a complete series of illustrated cards. The image could also be blown up or reduced so it might appear as a poster or letter heading (or both). The image could then be tried in lots of colour combinations. And if a colour printer is available the image could be printed to the appropriate size and then stuck on to an old credit card.

2 Marketing

This means making the card attractive to consumers and making them want to use it.

You could ask telephone card users for their likes and dislikes. This will help you to produce a phone card which might satisfy the consumer. However, it is worth remembering that your survey of consumers might not always be very representative.

The more attractive your card the less likely it is that it will be thrown away. Another idea would have been to specify limited editions and cards which have a theme to them. Rather like postage stamps, they may then become collectable.

There are several other factors to bear in mind apart from the specifications laid down in the competition. The card also needs to be safe, so make sure there are no jagged edges. If you have made the card properly and there are no edges it should fit quite nicely into the standard issue credit card holder.

The company's image is another point to consider. In a 'high-tech' industry a modern 'go-ahead' image is important, so your phone card should be in keeping with this style. Olde-English lettering and rose-patterned designs may therefore not be the most appropriate!

Stelaphone phone card competition

Overleaf are four entries to the Stelaphone Phone Card Competition. Assume you are one of the competition judges who has to put the entries in rank order (first to last). These entries are not the best ones possible but they are not totally useless. Each of them contains at least one good idea. Using the form provided assess each card in turn listing both the design faults and the good ideas. Entry 1 has been completed to give you some idea.

1

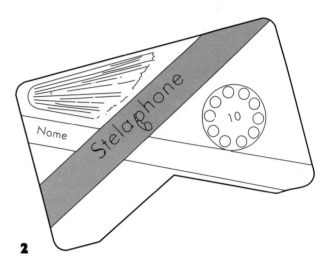

2

3

4

STELAPHONE PHONE CARD COMPETITION

OFFICIAL JUDGING FORM

✔ = GOOD SOLUTION   ✗ = POOR SOLUTION   O = NO SOLUTION

Design Specification

ENTRY No.	Std. Size	Ease of use	Unit count	Ident. func.	Count. logo	Attrac-tive	Comp. logo	After use	Design faults	Good points	Comments
1	✔	✗	O	✔	✔	✔	✔	✔	Incom-plete	Keyring refund idea	Hole in the wrong corner
2											
3											
4											

LONGER ASSIGNMENT 4: NOVELTY CAKE

Identifying needs and opportunities

Imagine that it is a friend's birthday. You want to do something different – make him a personal novelty cake! However, you want to make it relevant to one of his hobbies or interests and you want to make it so that it looks and tastes good!

If you don't have a birthday to celebrate perhaps it could be for another occasion such as passing a driving test. You could also think about a seasonal celebration such as Easter or Hallowe'en. You should of course discuss it with your parents because the cake will cost over £3.00 to produce. As a design exercise it has a lot going for it. However you will need permission and help from an adult. If it is not possible to produce the cake perhaps you could buy a plain one and then set about turning it into an original design.

Generating a design

One of the most challenging aspects of this exercise is deciding what you might model. You should start by considering two factors:

1 The importance of the object(s) to the person or the event.
2 How successfully the object could be modelled.

1 Choosing a relevant object

If you are creating a cake for a particular person then it should take the form of something closely associated with that person. It could perhaps be a valued personal possession such as a crash helmet, a computer or even a pair of trainers.

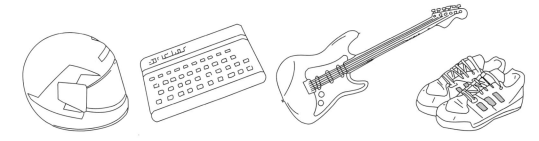

Below are a few examples which might get you thinking. Fill in 5, 6 and 7 with ideas of your own. This should trigger some thoughts on possible designs.

Hobbies	Associated items	Associated clothes	Themes
1 Music	Guitar Midi-system Personal stereo	Promotional wear	Pop group tour
2 Clothes	Wardrobe Chest of drawers 'Bum bag'	T-shirts Bermuda shorts Masks	Uniform Informal dress Fancy dress
3 Sport (hockey)	Sports bag Hockey stick and ball	Sports wear Protective kit	
4 Cars	Steering wheel Road wheel Tool box	Driving gloves	Passing driving test Repair
5			
6			
7			

2 How to successfully model the object

Now you will have to assess the items you have listed in terms of feasibility and visual effect. Consider a video recorder as an example. It is perfectly possible to make a cake in such a shape (e.g. a rectangle) which could then be decorated to represent buttons and visual displays. The visual effect, however, may not be particularly good, and there are a number of reasons for this. They are:

- There is no novelty value, the shape is a conventional cake shape and therefore not particularly unusual.
- Video recorders tend to be very plain and flat-sided which makes for a very uninteresting shape.

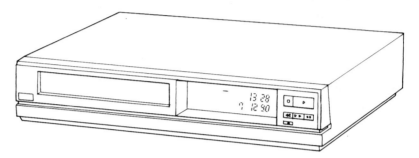

- It also means that the controls would have to be represented by decoration. This would mean they would be flat rather than solid.

Alternatively, if you choose to model a giant personal stereo, the main component of which is also a rectangle, this could be visually far more interesting. One major reason for this is the considerable variety in size, shape and texture of the components. The cable, headset, and player would not only exaggerate variety by contrast but they would also provide interesting opportunities in terms of modelling. Using liquorice for the cable and brightly coloured liquorice sweets for the earphones are examples of how you could exercise your creativity in thinking of appropriate materials.

Two other important reasons why this would be an interesting idea are:

- A change of scale has occurred, people would view a familiar object in an unfamiliar scale.
- A change of material has occurred, people would view a familiar object in an unfamiliar material.

In the past these points have been developed into techniques and used by artists such as Salvador Dali, René Magritte and Claes Oldenburg. These artists, along with many others, worked in a style which became known as 'surrealism'. All of them used the techniques described to confront their public with scenes which deliberately did not make sense or were even impossible to resolve. The effect was to hold people's interest through intrigue.

Salvador Dali, for example, would paint giant pocket watches in a way that made them look as if they were melting. René Magritte also painted everyday objects such as an apple or a comb but which had undergone a massive change in scale and were shown filling an entire room. Claes Oldenburg produces huge three-dimensional objects, such as a giant electric fan, in soft materials.

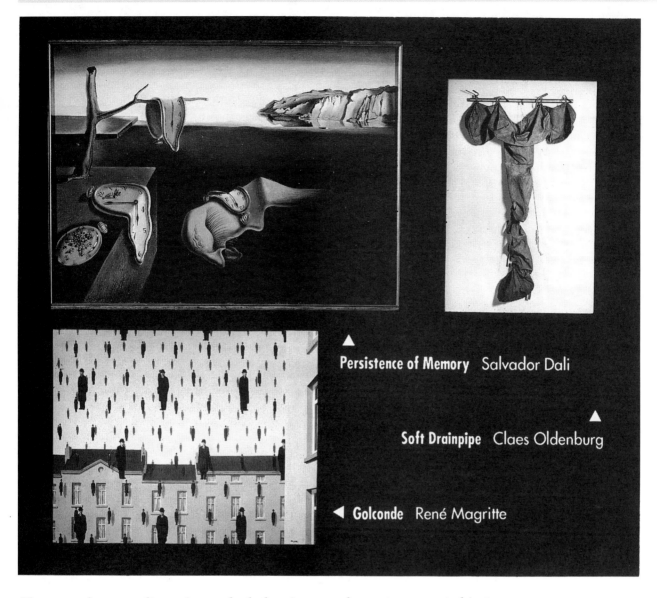

Persistence of Memory Salvador Dali

Soft Drainpipe Claes Oldenburg

◄ **Golconde** René Magritte

However the surrealist artist worked, the aim was always to present objects or images of objects that were out of context, that were in places or scales that were totally unexpected. This use of 'juxtaposition', as it is called, caused the onlooker to question reality. So, in baking a novelty cake you are dealing with the same abstract concepts as some of this century's most successful artists.

Another major factor governing the feasibility of your design is how well it lends itself to the choice of materials. The exact recipe for the cake will be discussed in detail in the next section but you must at this stage think hard about the qualities of the materials. The kind of questions you need to ask are:

- How strong is the material under tension (being pulled)?
- How strong is the material under compression (being squashed)?
- Can it support its own weight?
- Will the material gain or lose rigidity (stiffness) when it is baked?
- What kind of shapes can it be formed into?
- How long will it stay fresh?

Icing is a completely different material from the cake mixture and will therefore have different properties. It is known to be a 'plastic' material. This means that the material offers little resistance to changes in shape, form and texture. As a result materials which have this 'plastic' quality can be used to imitate other materials. This has in the past been the case with clay and also more recently plastic. This is because plastic can be made to imitate a wide variety of other materials. As a result of this it was thought to have no distinctive qualities of its own. It is only relatively recently that plastic has become valued as a material in its own right.

There are several types of icing you could make. But the design you are developing may need specific modelling qualities found only in one certain type. Thus there is a need for some research. Limit your investigations to three basic types and decide what are the important qualities. You may wish to draw up a chart similar to the one below which could help you to make easy comparisons.

	Icing type A	Icing type B	Icing type C
Cost	High	Moderate	Low
Taste	Sweet/sugary	Creamy/buttery	Sugary
Ease of making	Complicated/ would need assistance	Straightforward	Complicated/ need to follow instructions
Method of application	Spread with a knife, can be piped	Rolled out and applied in sheet form	Spread with a knife, can be piped
Finished effect	Rough but remains soft	Smooth, dries hard	Smooth, remains soft

The three types of icing are royal, butter and fondant. However, the descriptions listed above have all been jumbled up and so do not accurately describe each one of these particular types of icing. Try to sort them out into the correct order. Check your answer against the corrected chart shown on page 163.

 Having decided on the type of icing you would like to use you may then decide on some additional decoration. Obviously anything you use should not be toxic and must be thoroughly cleaned. The decorations could, of course, be edible. The vast selection of sweets available today means that it is possible to represent almost anything. For example, wood could be represented by flaked chocolate or wafers, ice by clear mints, cables by liquorice and LEDs or jewels by fruit gums. The list is endless, all you need to do is stand in front of a sweet counter and consider each product in turn!

Before attempting to design your own cake look at the design analysis below where you should consider the examples and then complete the preliminary design exercise. This will help you to broaden your understanding enabling you to adapt your design to meet the limitations of the materials you are using.

Design analysis

On the next few pages there are a number of designs which you should assess. None of the ideas as they appear has been completely thought through, some of them with a little more effort could be very good. Consider each idea in turn and complete the statements of criticism given by adding the most appropriate word from the choice given. Then look at the development of these ideas (illustrations on pages 157 to 158) to see if you think they have been improved.

Design 1

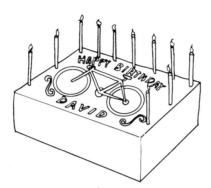

The shape is not at all unusual, it is far too	flat, even, regular, big
Not enough .... have been included in the design.	shapes, objects, components, forces
The decoration acts like a picture, it does not .... the shape of the cake.	fit, relate to, belong to, enlarge

Design 2

The structure would not .... itself.	colour, support, keep together, hold
The design could be further improved by including more	weight, pattern, objects, parts
.... could be put in the	Objects, Colours
.... of the toy.	back, front

Design 3

This design is not ....

safe, rigid, stable, big

The problem could be solved by choosing

a cup of a different ....

kind, shape, outline, texture

More .... would also make it more interesting.

weight, textures, components, objects

Answers

Best choice   *Worst choice*

Design 1

regular	even	flat	big
components	objects	shapes	forces
relate to	belong to	fit	enlarge

Design 2

support	keep together	hold	colour
objects	parts	pattern	weight
Objects			Colours
back			front

Design 3

stable	safe	rigid	big
shape	outline	kind	texture
components	objects	textures	weight

The most appropriate answer is on the left, the least appropriate is on the right. In the first answer, therefore, 'regular' is the best choice but 'even' is better than 'flat'. 'Big' is the worst choice of word.

What improvements could be made? The toy truck and the cup and saucer could be improved despite the criticisms made. If you examine the drawing of the truck on the next page you will see that three features have been added. You might consider whether the additions are an improvement or not. It could be that by trying to solve one problem another has been created.

The drawing of the cup and saucer shows that new features have also been created. These certainly give more variety and add visual impact but what other concerns do they raise?

Spoon has been added

Cup is of a different shape

Biscuits have been added

Once you have designed your novelty cake the next step is to decide how you are actually going to produce it. A good way of doing this is to draw your chosen object and then consider it in terms of its basic shapes. Look at the examples which follow and you will appreciate how what might seem to be a very complex shape, can often be just one or two shapes repeated a number of times.

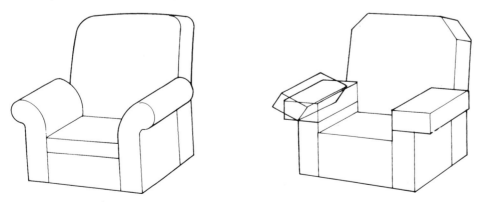

In the first example the easy chair could be assembled from a series of shapes cut from a cake baked in a large flat container, such as a roasting tin, and then bonded together with jam or cream. Of course the container need not be a roasting tin. Plant pots, baked bean tins and dishes could all be used providing you have permission, they are perfectly clean and you are sure they will not be damaged by the heat of the oven.

In the case of the marooned astronauts a pudding basin has been used for the end of the rocket while the remainder of the ship has been produced by cutting round appropriate sized objects such as cups, glasses and jars. Alternatively, a Swiss roll could be bought and used.

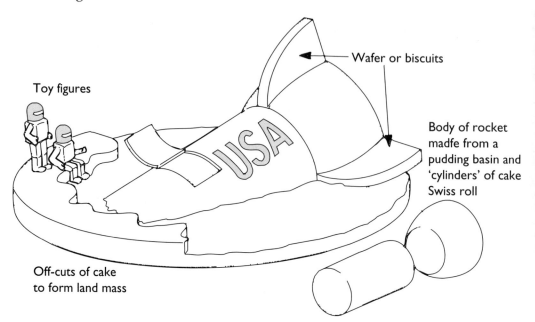

Toy figures

Wafer or biscuits

Body of rocket madfe from a pudding basin and 'cylinders' of cake Swiss roll

Off-cuts of cake to form land mass

The joystick could be produced in a similar way, with the addition of a skewer to add rigidity.

In all of these examples it is a case of analysing the original shape and then thinking what you might use as a mould in order to reproduce that shape. Or can you carve the shapes you require?

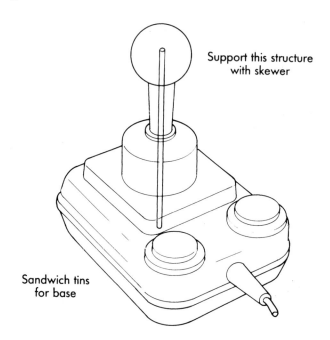

Support this structure with skewer

Sandwich tins for base

Another valuable preliminary exercise would be to model your idea, perhaps using plastic building bricks or card and plasticine. By doing this first you could try different sizes and proportions until you were satisfied you had them absolutely right.

Planning and making

Having developed your idea into a design you should now set about planning its production. This can be done in stages:

Stage 1   Identify and perhaps modify the recipe, collect together instructions, ingredients and equipment including appropriately shaped baking tins. Mix the ingredients and bake the cake.

Stage 2   This involves carving and modelling the material (the cake) in order to assemble the basic shape of the object you wish to represent.

Stage 3   Collect together instructions, ingredients and equipment in order to produce the icing and then decorate the cake.

Let's have a look at these in more detail.

Stage 1

When selecting a recipe you need to consider some of the following criteria:

– cost
– taste
– weight
– texture
– density
– colour

There are of course many different types of cake recipe available and most cooks have their own particular favourite. Perhaps you know someone who could help? Simple shapes could be produced from a fruit cake but more complex shapes requiring carving and assembly would require qualities found only in a certain type of sponge cake.

It is not possible to reproduce all the different types of recipes here so instead the various ingredients have been listed together with an explanation of their function. This should enable you to assess different recipes and identify the most appropriate.

Flour – the main 'structural' ingredient. For a light cake with a tender crumble a weak flour is required. Self-raising flour gives good results with simple recipes, using up to 1/2 fat to flour. For richer cakes plain flour is used with varying amounts of baking powder.

Sugar – sweetens a cake but it can also make it softer or more tender. Too much sugar will cause a cake to sink in the middle. Golden syrup may be used as a substitute for some of the sugar.

Fat – helps a cake to keep moist but it can also make it short and rich. Fat and sugar (caster) can be made to hold air when they are creamed together. Fat and sugar are most often used in equal quantities. If sugar exceeds fat the cake will be tender and spongy. If there is more fat than sugar it will be richer and closer (more solid and less crumbly) in texture.

Eggs – are very important in cake recipes because of the way they can be used to hold air in the mixture. They also add fat and give the cake a yellow colour. The more eggs the more air can be held and so the lighter the cake will be.

Liquids – milk and water both produce steam during cooking which helps to raise the cake. Gluten is also developed which helps to toughen the cake. Milk would of course add steam and fat.

Depending on your specific design you should now be able to decide on the kind of properties necessary to make your cake. If you have a particular recipe you wish to use compare it with the one below, and look at both against the above information to see which would be the most suitable to bake. To compare both recipes accurately you need to find the amount of ingredients per egg; you may therefore have to divide the quantities in your recipe by the number of eggs specified in your recipe.

Madeira Cake

For each egg:
50 g (2 oz) butter or margarine
50 g (2 oz) caster sugar
50 g (2 oz) self-raising flour
25 g (1 oz) plain flour
5 ml (one teaspoon) lemon juice
grated rind of 1/2 lemon

To give you some idea about sizes and quantities a four-egg mixture will fill a large roasting tin (28 × 18 × 4 cm). Alternatively, this mixture would fill a 20 cm round tin to a depth of about 8-10 cm.

Instructions
Below are a few basic instructions and tips for you to follow. However, it is recommended that you refer to more detailed instructions found in cookery books and magazines.

1 Prepare a cool oven (325°F, 160°C, gas mark 3).
2 Cream butter and sugar together until light and fluffy.
3 Beat eggs together and gradually add to the mixture, beating well after each addition. Sift flours together and fold into the creamed mixture with the lemon rind and juice.
4 Turn into a greased and lined cake tin and level the top. Bake until well risen, firm to touch and golden brown. Cooking time will vary according to the size and shape of the baking tins. As a guide a six–eight egg mixture will take about one and a quarter hours.
5 Remove from oven, allow to cool for 10 minutes then turn onto a wire rack.

Stage 2

You should first ensure you have assembled all the appropriate tools and materials. If your design requires a lot of cutting and joining then perhaps you should consider the bonding material(s) you are to use. You may be able to improve both appearance and taste by using more than one. You need to work on clean wipe-down surfaces, being prepared for a bit of a mess, particularly if there is a lot of carving to do.

Once you have started to cut the material you will realize its potential strengths and weaknesses and the consequent need for support. Work from the base upwards and outwards. Remember that the materials you are working with are fragile so handle both cake and icing materials gently.

Stage 3

Now it's time to do the icing. This is probably the most exciting part of this assignment! You should first ensure you have assembled all the appropriate tools and materials. Procedures will be different depending on the type of icing you have chosen.

Butter icings are not too difficult to make or handle. They can be spread quite easily with a palette or table knife after which the decorations can be added. This type of icing remains soft but if you require it to stiffen in order to hold certain decorations then put it in the fridge for a while.

Fondant icings require a little more care in preparation. You must first knead the icing, allowing the heat from your hands to soften the sugar. If, however, the icing remains too stiff to work then add a drop of egg white. If, on the other hand, the icing is too soft then add and mix in some more icing sugar. When rolling out fondant icing dust hands, surfaces and rolling pins well with icing sugar. Once the cake has been covered and the icing stretched and eased into shape it can be smoothed and polished by hand, although make sure the hand has been dusted in cornflour. Some cookery books recommend that you coat the cake with apricot jam before applying the icing in order to help the two stick together. Decorations can also be modelled in this icing, allowed to dry on greaseproofed paper and fixed to the surface by dampening adjoining surfaces.

Try to find out for yourself how to prepare and apply royal icing.

This has been a long and detailed assignment. However, if you have followed the guidelines correctly you should now be looking at a very successful piece of work, one which is a pleasure both to look at and to consume!

Evaluating

If you think back to the beginning of this assignment it should dawn on you that in actual fact you were presented with **two** challenges. The first of these was to make a suitable cake. However, you were also expected to successfully use the cake as modelling material.

The achievement of the former could be judged by the reaction of the recipient of the cake although good manners might preclude him or her from showing their true feelings if they disliked it! Perhaps a more objective judgment might be given by a parent or friend who may also have helped you. So ask them!

Sensible evaluation involves tests or trials, not only to assess taste but other factors such as texture, visual appearance and colour. These are the qualities concerned when actually eating the cake.

In this exercise other factors to consider are those associated with the second task: modelling the cake. This is about how easily it cuts and how well it retains its shape. If time permitted you might have undertaken a dry run and produced a prototype. Or you could have made occasional checks during preparation. For instance, you could have tested the quality of the cake yourself before completion by tasting it at one of the later stages of its preparation, e.g. during the mixing process. However, this should not have been done by the unhygienic method of sticking your finger in the mixture! Another occasion which allows interim testing is when the cake is cut into the various necessary shapes and some small pieces of cake fall off or are not needed. These could be eaten to check the taste.

The success of the modelling might have been indicated by the receiver's reactions. However, before giving the cake away you should compare it with the original specification. In the design stage you will probably have tried several different shapes and approaches. By discounting some and settling on a final version you have been testing your work. When you did the icing exercise earlier you were testing your knowledge in choosing the appropriate icing.

You will need to consider the procedure involved in the making of the novelty cake. Care, safety and the waste of materials will be general factors to bear in mind. Assuming there was suitable equipment available (e.g. a food mixer) you will need to comment on other (maybe better) alternatives. Similarly, you could consider if you used the equipment available to you in the most efficient way. For example, did you grease the baking tins so that the cake pieces came out cleanly, thereby minimizing waste?

In Stage 2 you needed to carve and the model the cake. You should ask yourself honestly whether or not your carving/modelling could be improved. The type of knife used might be important. For example, serrated edge knives are not usually used to cut cakes! In addition, the amount of wasted cake created should be measured.

A further problem which you should have considered is of storage. The relevant factors governing your decision are safety and temperature. You do not want your cake to be knocked over, or off the cooking racks. Furthermore, you do not wish the recipient to see it and thereby spoil the surprise. Also you do not want the cake to be exposed to very hot or very cold temperatures, so you will probably have put it in a secure container in the refrigerator.

One final point to consider is the total cost of this assignment. Remember your budget! Your costs need to include the raw materials such as ingredients, icing and decorations as well as indirect production costs such as the amount of electricity or gas used.

Can you think of any indirect costs?

They include lighting, rent and rates on the property. However, for the short amount of time which you have taken these costs would be so small that you can discount them.

There is however another cost to consider – namely your **time**! It is assumed at the start that your time was free. However, you could have been doing something else, and maybe earning money: baby sitting at £3.00 an hour, for example! You need to consider the cost of your time. This possible alternative use of time (which you gave up to make the cake) is called the 'opportunity cost' by economists. It is the alternative given up in order to do (or buy) something else.

INFORMATION TECHNOLOGY

Art/graphics

An art/DTP package could be used to produce high quality graphics which could accompany the cake. This could take the form of a greetings card or a banner to go round the base of the cake.

Data bases

These could be used to research and store cake recipes.

Spreadsheets

These could be used to calculate costs.

ICING DETAILS FROM PAGE 154

	Royal icing	Butter icing	Fondant icing
Cost	Moderate	High	Low
Taste	Sweet/sugary	Creamy/buttery	Sugary
Ease of making	Complicated/ would need assistance	Straightforward	Complicated/ need to follow instructions
Method of application	Spread with a knife, can be piped	Spread with a knife, can be piped	Rolled out and applied in sheet form
Finished effect	Smooth, dries hard	Rough but remains soft	Smooth, remains soft

LONGER ASSIGNMENT 5: BRIDGING THE GAP

BRIDGES

Although there may seem to be many different types of bridge existing today there are in fact only three basic types. These are classified according to their structure and are:

> **girder**
> **suspension**
> **arch**

These three basic types of bridge can be combined in many ways to suit individual situations. In a bridge a 'span' is the length between one pier or support and another, so a bridge of several spans can be used to create a passage across a wide river. If, however, the river is very deep, or has ships with tall masts sailing up and down it, then a long-span, high-level bridge may be needed. Arch and girder bridges are more rigid than suspension bridges and are better able to bear heavy loads such as railway trains.

Girder bridges

The first girder (sometimes called a beam) bridge was probably a tree that had fallen across a river. A development of this was the use of thinner lengths of material, criss-crossed together to form a 'truss'. This is the basis of the modern girder bridge and minimizes the amount of materials used. Girder bridges simply rest on the ground or if they are very long on intermediate supports.

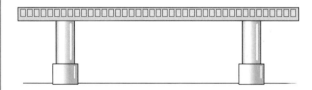

Suspension bridges

The second type of bridge to develop was probably the suspension bridge. This may have originated in tropical forests where vines and creepers could have been tied from one tree to another. Later a walkway would have been added. In this situation the creepers pull on the tree, which of course is able to resist because it is anchored to the ground by its roots.

A development of this type of bridge would have been the use of logs where no trees were available. In this case the logs would have been driven into the ground, but since they had no roots other anchorage points such as ropes and stakes had to be found. Suspension bridges **pull** on their supports, trying to force them closer together.

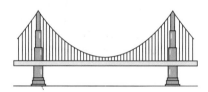

Arch bridges

The third type of bridge to consider is that based on one or more archways. Traditionally these bridges were constructed from stone cut into special wedge shapes. These stones were then positioned over a wooden former, until the last one (the key stone) was in place. This type of bridge is quite difficult to construct because, unlike a suspension bridge, the archway cannot support any part of itself until it is complete. In contrast to the suspension bridge, arch bridges thrust outwards and **push** on their supports (abutments), trying to force them further apart.

Identifying needs and opportunities

Imagine that a group of engineering firms are keen to support their industry by sponsoring annual competitions. In the past these competitions have been designed to promote the creative side of engineering by posing joke problems. One such task has been to design and produce from paper, a transport device for an egg. The device had to protect the egg from a fall of three metres and be capable of being dragged over a series of obstacles.

☆ COMPETITION ☆

Design and construct a bridge for model cars. The bridge must be made entirely out of paper!

Specification:
– bridge length 0.5 metre
– deck should be flat, at least 5cm wide
– bridge must not be supported from underneath or sides

| FIRST PRIZE | – | Weekend for two on Humberside including full guided tour of Humber Bridge. |
| TWO RUNNERS UP | – | A copy of *The World's Bridges*, just published |

From the stimulus material included it can be seen that this year the competition is about building a bridge out of newspaper. The bridge has to be 0.5 metres long and have a flat deck at least 5 cm wide that would allow model cars to travel along it. The bridge cannot be supported from underneath or the sides.

This project then is about structures and how they can best withstand stresses and strains while performing a specific function, in this case supporting a weight or 'load' across a gap. There is a great deal to learn in this assignment so you might want to tackle it with some friends.

One way of doing this is to work as a team with each member specializing in a certain aspect of the problem. Working on the principle that 'two heads are better than one' this would allow you to share ideas and negotiate solutions. This is how things happen in the real world. Even relatively simple things such as children's toys involve teams of designers with each member specializing in areas such as development, production techniques, assembly, packaging and marketing. Consider for a moment then how many teams of designers would be involved in creating a power station or an oil refinery.

An extension of the team idea is to develop the project as a competition between friends and relatives. If you choose to do this then you would have to develop the lists below into rules, in order for each team to have the same resources and therefore the same chances of success.

Even if you do not attempt this project as a competition it is a good idea to impose limits on yourself. In the real world it is a poor designer who uses materials needlessly for it increases costs and squanders the earth's resources.

Listed below are the materials needed to complete this project and suggestions as to how they might be limited:

- 10, 15 or 20 sheets of regular sized newspaper
- one metre of tape (preferably the type called 'masking tape')
- a pair of scissors
- a thin knitting needle (or something similar that you can use to wrap newspaper round)
- paper and pencil

Also needed is a design brief, a specification the bridge has to meet and an agreed means by which it will be tested.

Let us start by saying that:

- the bridge has to span a gap of 0.5 of a metre
- it has to have a flat deck at least 5 cm wide
- when loaded the middle of the bridge should not distort any more than 2 cm
- it must withstand the load for at least one minute
- it has to be completed in a given time

Material properties

There are then two aspects to this project that need to be considered simultaneously. The first thing that needs to be done is an investigation of the properties of the materials to be used. At first you might think that a bridge made from newspaper might not be able to stand a great deal of stress in the form of weight. However, if you conduct your investigations correctly you should develop the means by which a considerable weight can be supported.

Construction methods

Having developed some understanding of how to use the materials available, you can look at the second aspect of this project which is to develop a design that uses the specific qualities of the materials to maximum effect. Bearing in mind that newspaper can, like concrete and steel, be used in a variety of different ways, a good start would be to consider different types of bridge construction . This will give some idea how various shapes and methods of construction differ in the way they are able to withstand and spread loads.

Let us start by investigating the materials in some depth. We should begin by considering that while newspaper can be laminated (sheets stuck together in layers like toilet tissue or plywood) it also needs to be fashioned in such a way that it offers structural rigidity. The most effective way of achieving this quality is to fashion the newspaper into thin, hollow rods or tubes. It might take a little practice to develop the knack of producing these tubes but in doing so you should learn something about the material and how slight differences in production affect final strength.

Planning and making
Producing the tubes or hollow rods

Start by tearing off some pieces of adhesive tape about 5 cm long and attaching them temporarily to the edge of a large, flat working surface. Then place a sheet of newspaper on the surface, directly in front of you, so that a corner is pointing towards you.

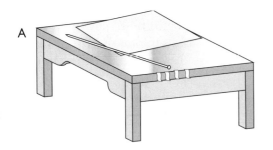 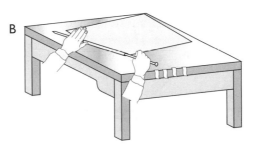

Now you need to use a knitting needle (or something similar such as a very long thin pencil) as a former. Around this you will wrap the newspaper. Place the knitting needle across the corner of the paper nearest to you, wrapping the tip of the paper tightly around it. Then, still holding the paper so it does not loosen, and using the fingers and palm of one hand, roll the former away from you. Stop once you have gone past your thumb. Now, using your spare hand to maintain the tension on the tube, reposition your rolling hand so that you are able to repeat the process. You may have to pull the needle out as you go along.

Continue this process until the tube is complete, using a piece of adhesive tape to secure the exposed end. Once you have got the process started you will be able to remove the knitting needle since the tube will be strong enough to support itself.

The key to producing strong tubes is to keep the newspaper under constant pressure. As the length of the rod increases you will need to use both hands to roll the former, maintaining the tension on the newspaper with one hand at all times. That then is the process. With a little practice you should soon develop the technique. The next task is to investigate how differences in production techniques affect final strength.

As we have already learnt, **tension** is an important factor governing strength. This is because it acts like a glue, holding the layers firmly together. If the diameter of the tube is increased, to say that of a rolling pin (5-6 cm), then not only would the number of layers of newspaper be decreased, thereby reducing the thickness of the tube wall, but the individual layers would be free to slide over one another. This would greatly lessen their strength.

Another factor that determines strength is the **angle** of the former as it lies across the newspaper. Try producing a tube with the former square to one edge and then compare this to one where the former is positioned at a very steep angle.

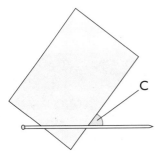 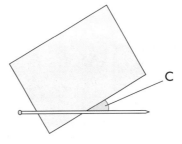

These tubes will have different qualities because of the angle at C.

With a selection of different tubes varying in size and wall thickness there is now a need to assess their individual **strengths**. At the simplest level this could be done by flexing the different tubes between your hands. Unfortunately this is not very scientific and makes comparisons quite difficult. More accurate results could be achieved by suspending **weights** of increasing amounts from a tube, while the tube is spanning a gap. Another test could be to loop an elastic band over the tube and then stretch one end, measuring the length on the elastic band regularly up to the point of collapse. These tests assess the strength of the tubes in one direction. There are, however, other ways in which you will want to use the tubes and these should also be investigated.

Depending on how you have constructed the tubes, some should be quite strong along their length and so should not yield when being stretched. They could therefore be used to suspend loads. Alternatively the tubes should be able to withstand being compressed (provided you cut off the ends where the walls are very thin). Used in this way the tubes could withstand a considerable force but you will need to know differences in performance, that is between **tension** and **compression**, since this will have an important impact on your design. Compression tests could be carried out using a set of bathroom scales.

As a general rule you should find that the tubes offer the greatest strength when being stretched along their length, that is when under tension. The tubes can also withstand loads when being compressed, although there are problems in ensuring the stress is spread evenly down the tube.

The tubes are weak when stress is applied in **one place**, particularly if the stress acts across the diameter of the tube. This causes the tube to distort and **when it loses its shape it also loses its strength**. The key to building a strong structure therefore is not to allow the tubes to distort. To increase the load a tube can withstand you have to prevent the tube from buckling.

The use of tubes in the bicycle industry

Manufacturing light tubes and making strong joints with them has been a major consideration of the bicycle industry for many years. Until recently it was thought that the bicycle would become a thing of the past since everybody would have a car. In fact today there are more bicycles made than at any other time in the past. This is because people are much more health conscious. In response to this manufacturers are producing fun machines, particularly the 'mountain bike'.

This particular type of bicycle has to be very strong but at the same time very light in weight. This has demanded a new approach to bicycle design, particularly in the frame. To prevent this from snapping and buckling manufacturers have come up with several solutions. If you have a look around the bicycle racks when you are at school you should be able to see some of them.

Of course some of these solutions, such as using stronger materials, cannot be seen. Neither is it possible to see how some manufacturers have made the tube walls thicker in certain places. This is because they have made the walls thicker on the inside. On the outside the tube looks the same thickness all the way along its length.

Other developments are obvious. One of these has been to increase the diameter of certain tubes – that is the ones that take the most strain. The 'down tube', for example, connects the pedals to the handlebars and is now on some bikes twice as fat as the other tubes. Other designs incorporate more than one shape of tube. Traditionally all tubes were round in cross section but now square and oval tubes are to be seen in some frames. This is because these shapes are thought to offer greater rigidity. Oval tubes are used because more strength is required in one direction than another.

These then are some of the ways that designers think mountain bikes should look. Of course you have to remember that 'fashion' or 'image' is also a major aspect of design. Some bikes are made to look different for the sake of it rather than because of increased strength.

Joining the tubes

Whatever structure you eventually design the chances are that the tubes will need to be joined together. There is therefore a need to investigate how this can best be done. Remember what we have learnt about the strength of the tubes and that preserving the shape would preserve the strength. Think also about mountain bike manufacture and the idea of thickening the tube in places where extra strength is needed, then consider the two sketches below. Of course you cannot thicken the tube on the inside but you can thicken it in another way. Look again at the two sketches and you should be able to see that one joint offers greater support than the other. Here is the key to creating strong joints.

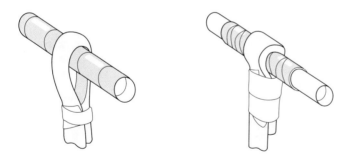

Generating a design

With some understanding of the strength of your materials some thought should now be given to structures and which ones will best suit your needs. Probably the oldest means of bridging a gap was to use a long log. In fact you could develop this idea yourself and simply tape your tubes together in a bundle, creating a honeycomb structure.

Although this could be an excellent method of constructing the deck, used on its own, it would not be the strongest structure you could produce. A carefully designed structure, utilising this idea with methods of spreading and transferring loads into the ground would be very much more successful.

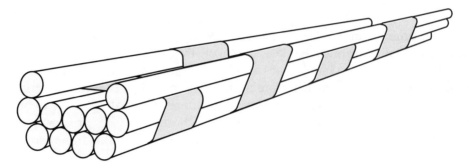

One important lesson all designers have to learn is not to reinvent the wheel. This is because it already exists. Therefore do not try to start your design from scratch. Instead consider the information given in the panel on 'Bridges' and then look at the illustrations. These are bridges that already exist. Each one solves a design problem by using the materials in the most effective way.

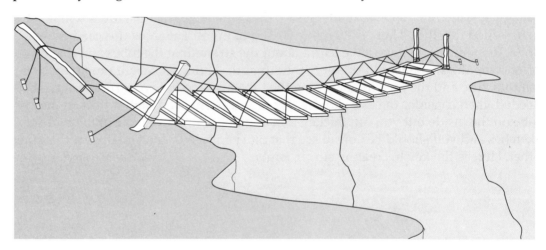

Look at the rope bridge; this was probably the second form of bridge to be developed. Now imagine you have been given the job of strengthening it. The only materials available to you are rope and logs. Look at the bridge and imagine that an enormous weight (such as several horses with huge sacks on their backs) is in the middle. Ask yourself questions about how the weight or load is transferred along the ropes to the logs which act as anchorage points. Then complete the statements below by choosing the most appropriate word from those given.

Now test yourself

In order to increase the strength of the bridge the ropes that attach to the logs and stakes have to be made (1) .... This could be achieved by (2) .... two ropes together to form one big rope and then replacing them one at a time. This will allow the bridge itself to take additional loads and transfer them to the anchorage points.

The next thing to consider is that, if the ropes do not snap, the only way that the bridge can fail is if the (3) .... fail. This could

happen in two ways. One thing that could happen is that the logs and stakes could (4) ....
or .... The other possibility is that they might be pulled out of the ground. The logs and stakes could also be made (5) .... to prevent them from failing. There are other ways in which the strength of the anchorage could be increased. One way would be to increase the (6) .... of them. That is instead of having just one stake to each rope, two additional stakes could be used to secure the original one (see diagram).

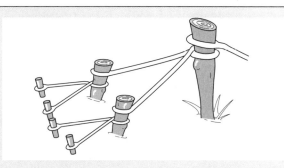

(1) thicker, thinner, lighter, heavier

(2) sewing, binding, gluing, tying

(3) anchorage points, ropes, rocks

(4) twist, stretch, snap, bend, melt

(5) thicker, thinner, lighter, heavier

(6) shape, weight, number, colour

(7) place, speed, angle

(8) out of, into

(9) loops, triangles, straight lines

(10) watching, helping, resisting, transferring

(11) opposite, similar

(12) out, along, beneath, further into

(13) thinner, stronger, longer, fatter

Another point to consider is the (7) .... at which the stakes are driven into the ground. In the original illustration some of the stakes are at the wrong angle. That is the forces applied, from weight on the bridge, are trying to pull them (8) ....the ground. The forces are acting in (9) ....through the ropes and stakes and have nothing (10) .... them. However, if you look at the diagram again you will see that other stakes are driven into the ground at the (11)........................... angle. This means that the forces acting on the stake are in fact working to pull the stakes (12) .... the ground. The final point about making the anchorage points stronger is to make the stakes (13)........................... so they could be driven further into the ground.

See answers on p.174

Evaluation

If you compare the illustration of the Humber Bridge with that of the rope bridge you will be able to see similarities and differences. Both structures are similar in that the deck is suspended from the main cables or ropes and in both cases these cables or ropes are suspended from towers or logs. If you compare the anchorage points you will also be able to see that the principles of security are the same. It is only the scale and the materials that differ.

There is, however, one important difference in the design of these two structures and this is in the shape of the decks. Consider the materials and shape of the deck in the rope bridge and, in your mind's eye, draw two arrows to indicate the direction of the stresses when the bridge is under load. Now do the same with the illustration of the Humber Bridge.

Now test yourself

In the case of the rope bridge the stresses are pulling from the (1)........................... , where the main logs are positioned, towards the (2)........................... of the bridge. Now consider the Humber Bridge. Here, because the deck is rigid and because of its different shape, the stresses are transmitted in the opposite direction – that is from the (3)........................... towards the (4)........................... . This is very important because it means that the deck is no longer having to withstand all the loads as dead weight. Some of the load is now transmitted along the deck into where it meets the ground.

(1) edges, sides, top, bottom

(2) back, middle, side, centre

(3) back, front, top, bottom, middle

(4) top, bottom, edges, sides

See answers on p.174

This last point is the principle of the arch and the means by which many stone structures support themselves and the loads they have to carry. During construction all archways need support but once the keystone is in position the archway transmits all loads to the sides. In some cases the sides are natural supports, as in the case of a river bank, while in others stone towers have to be built.

Hard ground is needed for both **suspension** and **arch** bridges. This is to ensure that the abutments (main towers and anchorage points) can, without moving or giving way, withstand all the forces that are pulling and pushing on them. On soft ground it would be wiser to construct one or a series of **girder** bridges.

The type of girder bridge suitable for long spans is the **cantilever** bridge. One of the most famous of these types is the Forth Railway Bridge in Scotland. Here the huge balanced spans, each over 500 metres long, were designed to give the appearance of great strength. In this kind of structure the weight and stress of one side of the bridge is counterbalanced by the forces acting on the other side.

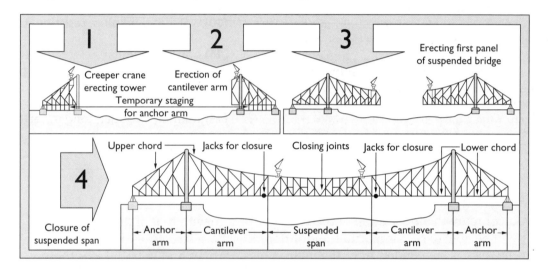

Of course there are many other types of bridges in the world, such as the wooden trestle.

The **suspension** bridge illustrated on p.72 is the Humber Bridge, at present the longest single-span suspension bridge in the world. When it was built it was a great engineering feat and even today some of the statistics remain very impressive.

HUMBER BRIDGE: FACTS AND FIGURES

Main span	1,410m
Side spans, North	280m
South	530m
Total length between anchorages	2,220m
Clearance over high water	30m
Carriageways Dual two-lane carriageway plus	
separate footpaths	
Total deck width	
(including footpaths)	28.5m
Tower height above piers	155.5m
Main cables Two cables, each of 14,948 wires	
of 5mm diameter plus an	
additional 800 similar wires	
in each cable on the Hessle side	
Diameter of main cables	0.68m
Total length of wire	71,000km
Load in each cable	19,400 tonnes
Weight of steel:	
deck structure	16,500 tonnes
main cables	11,000 tonnes
Total weight of concrete	480,000 tonnes
Depth of foundations:	
Anchorage, North side	21m
Anchorage, South side	35m
Tower, North side	8m
Tower, South side	36m

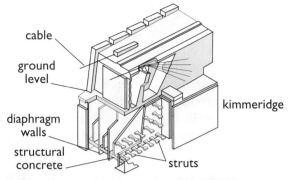

Concrete struts between diaphragm walls

The Humber Bridge has the longest single span of any bridge in the world and represents a considerable achievement for British engineering design and construction. Below is a table of the main span lengths of the world's great suspension bridges:

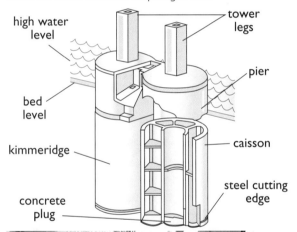

NAME	COUNTRY	SPAN (METRES)	YEAR OF OPENING TO TRAFFIC	CARRIAGE-WAY WIDTH (METRES)
Humber	England	1410	1981	18.2
Verrazano Narrows	U.S.A.	1298	1964	25.3
Golden Gate	U.S.A.	1280	1937	25.0
Mackinac	U.S.A.	1158	1957	16.0
Mihami Bison Seto	Japan	1100	1988	22.5
Bosporus II	Turkey	1090	1988	30.8
Bosporus I	Turkey	1074	1973	28.0
George Washington	U.S.A.	1067	1931	–
25th April Bridge	Portugal	1013	1967	16.0
Akashi Kaikyo	Japan	1990	1998*	30.0
Great Belt	Denmark	1624	1993	23.6
Tsing Ma	Hong Kong	1377	1993	30.7

*Anticipated opening date

Whilst no dates for construction are available, the longest span bridge in the world known to be under consideration is a bridge across the Straits of Messina, linking Calabria (Italy) to Sicily. This bridge, if built, will have a single span of 3,300 metres.

A portal beam being built into the tower

From looking at the illustrations and evaluating the work done so far you should now be able to start to design your bridge.

As a result of the tests and by studying the basic types of bridge construction it should be obvious that the arch bridge does not really suit the characteristics of the specified materials. Paper tubes will buckle rather than assume a natural arch. We are therefore left to consider the girder and suspension bridge for ideas. Look again at the diagrams and try to identify simple geometric shapes that occur regularly. Think also about natural structures and the idea of a honeycomb deck. Good luck!

Answers to Now test yourself

Page 170–171

(1) thicker
(2) binding
(3) anchorage points
(4) snap, bend or stretch
(5) thicker
(6) number
(7) angle
(8) out of
(9) straight lines
(10) resisting
(11) opposite
(12) further into
(13) longer

Page 171

(1) edges
(2) middle
(3) middle
(4) edges

Glossary

Aesthetic	Appreciating beauty.
Analysis	To break down into smaller parts.
Artefacts	Objects made by people.
Bought-in	Purchased ready-made components.
Bradawl	A woodworker's tool used to make small holes in timber.
CAD	Computer Aided Design.
CAM	Computer Aided Manufacturing.
Conductor	Capable of passing electricity or heat.
Constraints	The limits which influence your design decisions.
Contexts	Certain circumstances.
Data base	A collection of information.
Design brief	Short statement of problem.
Design capability	The ability to design technological things.
Design process	Stages in designing something.
Economics	Management of money.
Environments	Surroundings developed by people.
Evaluating	Judging.
Field	Part of a spreadsheet.
Graphics	Artwork.
Hypothesis	Like a theory.
Indirect cost	Costs which are not obvious.
Insulator	Able to prevent the passing of electricity or heat.
LED	Light emitting diode.
Malleable	Capable of being distorted without the material fracturing.
Marketing	The process whereby a product is 'sold' to the public.
Market research	Establishing how people feel about products or services.
Market segment	A selected or specialized part of a market.
Mass production	Automatic process created to produce unlimited numbers of an item.
One-off	When you intend to make only one of a design.
Opportunity cost	The cost of an alternative given up for something else.
Production sequence	Order in which something is made.
Prototype	Original model.
Researching	Careful search for information.
Scale of production	The number of an item you intend to produce.
Specification	A detailed list of the requirements of a design solution.
Spreadsheet	A table of information upon which calculations are made.
Surrealism	A form of art with unusual images linked together.
Symmetrical	A pattern where one part is perhaps a mirror image of another.
Systems	A set of objects which perform a task.
Template	A shaped piece such as a sewing pattern.
Word processing	Writing on a computer.

Index